Togo, the Sled Dog

and Other Great Animal Stories of the North

Compiled and edited by
Joe L. Wheeler

PACIFIC PRESS® PUBLISHING ASSOCIATION
NAMPA, IDAHO
OSHAWA, ONTARIO, CANADA
WWW.PACIFICPRESS.COM

Cover art by Lars Justinen
Cover designed by Justinen Creative Group
Interior illustrations from the library of Joe L. Wheeler
Inside design by Aaron Troia

Additional copies of this book are available by calling toll-free 1-800-765-6955 or by visiting www.adventistbookcenter.com.

www.joewheelerbooks.com

Representing the author is WordServe Literary Group Ltd., 10152 Knoll Circle, Highland Ranch, CO 80130.

Library of Congress Cataloging-in-Publication Data:

Wheeler, Joe L., 1936-
Togo, the sled dog : and other great animal stories of the north /
compiled and edited by Joe L. Wheeler.
p. cm.—(The good Lord made them all)
ISBN 13: 978-0-8163-2431-6 (pbk.)
ISBN 10: 0-8163-2431-X (pbk.)
1. Sled dogs—Alaska—Biography. 2. Dogsledding—Alaska. 3. Dogsledding—
Canada, Northern. 4. Dogsledding—Arctic regions. 5. Animals—Arctic regions—
Anecdotes. I. Wheeler, Joe L., 1936-
SF428.7.W44 2011
636.73—dc22
2010033869

11 12 13 14 15 • 5 4 3 2 1

DEDICATION

Once upon a dog-time—well, actually, in 1913—there was born in Nome, Alaska, a Siberian puppy, offspring of Dolly (one of the fifteen Siberians purchased from Siberia as a proposed gift from Jafet Lindeberg to famed Arctic explorer, Roald Amundsen) and Suggen (Leonhard Seppala's famed lead dog during their three consecutive wins in the All Alaska Sweepstakes in 1915, 1916, and 1917).

Though colicky as an infant, and a constantly-in-trouble juvenile delinquent later on, this unlikely candidate for stardom quickly became Seppala's lead dog, the true hero of the Great Serum Run of 1925.

After all his well-earned honors, he was cruelly sabotaged by the Stateside press that mistakenly credited all his stellar achievements to another of Seppala's dogs, Balto. Even worse, for more than eighty-five years, the press/media refuses to correct that mistake. Only in Alaska is the true hero of the Great Serum Run acknowledged.

Thus we feel it is long past time to begin a correctional groundswell by dedicating this book of stories of the North to the greatest dog of them all:

TOGO

Other books in the series
The Good Lord Made Them All
by Joe L. Wheeler

Amelia, the Flying Squirrel
and Other Great Stories of God's Smallest Creatures

Dick, the Babysitting Bear
and Other Great Wild Animal Stories

Owney, the Post Office Dog
and Other Great Dog Stories

Smoky, the Ugliest Cat in the World
and Other Great Cat Stories

Spot, the Dog That Broke the Rules
and Other Great Heroic Animal Stories

Wildfire, the Red Stallion
and Other Great Horse Stories

Contents

INTRODUCTION

ALASKA'S IDITAROD

Joseph Leininger Wheeler

Its origins

They call it "The Last Great Race on Earth"—and it lives up to its name.

The story of the Iditarod Sled Dog Race is as improbable as the story of the Great Serum Run to Nome that inspired it. (It is told movingly in Lew Freedman's book, *Father of the Iditarod: The Joe Redington Story*).

It began when Joe Redington and his wife, Vi, found the call of the North to be impossible to resist, and moved from Pennsylvania to Alaska in 1948; here they homesteaded at Flat Horn Lake and settled down on Knik Arm just a few miles from Wasilla.

They say an institution is but the shadow of one person: one person with a dream. Redington's dream started with his discovery that the sled dog way of life was disappearing from Alaska. There were fewer and fewer dogs every day that passed. In their places were bright yellow snow machines. Soon the era of the sled dog would be but a memory.

Enter Dorothy Page, chair of the Alaska Centennial Purchase Committee. She chanced to ask Redington a question: "Do you think it would be possible to conduct a sled dog race on the old Iditarod Trail? Is enough of it still open or usable?" Joe said he thought so; after all, he and Vi mushed dogs on that trail almost every day. Page pounced, anointing him chairman of the Iditarod Trail Committee.

Joe just happened to be the one man in Alaska with the vision to take those two questions and transubstantiate them into the greatest race in the world. For her role in all this, and remaining on board for the rest of her life, Page is called "Mother of the Iditarod"; and he, "Father of the Iditarod."

According to Freedman, what Joe did was to take the All Alaska Sweepstakes sled dog race that during the years 1910–1917 transformed Nome into the "Dog Capital of the World," tie it to the epic Great Serum Race to Nome of 1925, then, when it appeared the dream would die stillborn, had the audacity to organize a thousand-mile sled race from Anchorage to Nome—no sled dog race of that length had ever taken place!—and offer a purse of $50,000! People everywhere not only thought he was crazy, they told him so. Howard Farley quipped that there wasn't $50,000 in prize money for all the dog races in the world combined! So where was all that money coming from?

Joe didn't have the faintest idea. He just had a sixth sense that only a dramatic thousand-mile race commemorating the Great Serum Race and the Old Iditarod Trail, beginning in Anchorage and ending in Nome, with a $50,000 purse, was big enough—perhaps staggering enough—to catch the imagination of Alaskans everywhere.

On March 2, 1973, thirty-four sled dog teams rushed away from the Anchorage Tudor Road starting point. Redington wasn't in it—he was still trying to raise the money for the purse at the other end. Finally, the $50,000 became a reality, but he had to take out a $30,000 loan on his house to pull it off.

The big question on everyone's mind was, *Would anyone actually finish the thing?* After all, it had never been done before. As to how long it would take, no one knew the answer to that either. Joe was so strapped for cash, they had to prepare a double-duty banner: one side for the starting point and the other for the ending of the race. Twenty-two teams made it to Nome. Dick Wilmarth won it in 20 days, 49 minutes, 41 seconds; John Schultz came in last (in 32 days), receiving the now legendary Red Lantern, the symbolic reward for the last musher in, meaning, "We're leaving the light on for you."

All Alaska celebrated. The impossible had happened—but would it ever happen again? When it did, people began marking it on their calendars.

In 1975, the Humane Society of the United States declared the race inhumane and did its best to kill it. Redington was outraged: it was common knowledge that not only did the dogs love it, they were in far better shape in Nome at the end than were the mushers.

Each year that followed was a struggle. Had it not been for Redington, it would long since have folded. He was always coming up with new ideas to publicize it and keep it alive.

In 1976, he came up with a two hundred dog-long sled team to celebrate America's bicentennial.

In 1978, Redington finally got a bill through Congress that added the 2,200-mile-long Iditarod Trail to the list of America's National Historic Trails.

In 1979, Redington, Susan Butcher, and Rob Stapleton mushed a sled dog team to the top of North America's highest mountain, 20,320-foot Mount McKinley. They experienced a terrific storm that almost blew them off the mountain; Susan Butcher's team almost ran away from her, saved only by their indefatigable guide, Ray Genet. Finally, on May 28, they and three of their dogs reached the very summit, from which they could see far-off Anchorage. The dogs, not tired at all, just looked around curiously for the rest of the trail. Stapleton quipped, "Joe had trained the dogs to go—they just hadn't been trained to stop." But they certainly had proved that dog teams had unbelievable stamina. It had taken them forty-four days to pull off what even most Alaskans considered an impossibility.

In 1982, Joe and Vi rode in a sled with small wheels in Reagan's Inaugural parade in Washington, D.C.

In 1983, they put on the seventy-fifth anniversary celebration of the first All Alaska Sweepstakes that made Iron Man Johnson, Scotty Allan, and Leonhard Seppala folk heroes.

But it was 1985 that meant the most for the race's future. Redington had long been nurturing women, encouraging them to compete in the Iditarod. Susan Butcher was well on her way to winning the race that year when her team was attacked by an angry moose, leaving her team and sled in shambles and several dogs killed. But Libby Riddles saved the day and won. With that, the press went crazy—finally an Iditarod cover girl!

Susan Butcher *did* make it, however, in 1986—also 1987, 1988, and 1990. All this predicably resulted in the best-selling Iditarod T-shirt ever, with these words in large letters: ALASKA, WHERE MEN ARE MEN AND WOMEN WIN THE IDITAROD.

Each year, the controversy for first place is fierce, making the winners household names in the sporting world. Names such as:

Rich Swenson	(5 times)	Jeff King	(4 times)
Susan Butcher	(4 times)	Lance Mackey	(4 times)
Martin Buser	(4 times)	Doug Swingley	(4 times)

By the 1990s, the Iditarod had become the best-known mushing event, not only in America, but around the world.

Another great dogsled race today is the Yukon Quest (it is run from Fairbanks to Whitehorse in Canada's Yukon).

But a lot of things have changed: it can now be run in just under ten days; mushers have food and supplies flown in to towns along the way; mushers are no longer permitted to bunk with villagers, but must rest in common facilities; everything is much faster paced than ever before; and the purse continues to grow.

Yet some things are unchanged. It is still the world's most unpredictable race, with blinding blizzards, plunging temperatures, overhanging branches, buffalo, moose, and wild cards of every kind guaranteeing it will never become formulaic. Mushers can still attend and participate from all over the world; mushers may move as slowly or as rapidly as they choose; they may still reminisce with each other around evening campfires; and best of all, they know that each race is a once-in-a-lifetime event that the whole world is watching. Oh not quite best of all—best of all, old-time mushers say—is *mushing a dog team under the stars, the only sound the padding of huskies' feet on the trail and the hiss of the sled runners.*

And yet how close a call it was! How grateful we must ever be that one man—Joe Redington—believed enough in his dream to build foundations under it that are standing the test of time. More significantly, by so doing, he rescued for you, me, America, and the world, one of the greatest legacies of the past—the sled-dog world.

Its dogs

I had always thought a musher was a musher, a dogsled was a dogsled, a sled dog was a sled dog, and the Iditarod was the Iditarod—until God gave me an epiphany in the middle of the night of May 26/27, 2010, and suddenly, the light came on: they all add up to one word—*dog.*

Up till then, the story of Seppala, Togo, and the Great Serum Run was just a story; now, with the epiphany, I realized for the very first time what I'd been missing: the canine ingredient. Without dogs, there would be no story at all. With dogs, a new item was added to my bucket list—*experience the Iditarod personally* with Connie *before we die.*

For the incredible yearly thousand-mile soap opera that is the Iditarod is neither more nor less than the lengthened shadow of one man and one dog: Leonhard Seppala and Togo, quite possibly the greatest dog who ever lived. I use the pronoun *who* deliberately, for Togo was far more than "just a dog," just as Seppala was far more than "just a man."

Connie and Joe Wheeler, Juneau, Alaska, at a sled-dog summer training camp.

More and more, over this past year, the epic story of the Great Serum Run of 1925 has obsessed me. I used to laugh at our cherished friend Bob Mendenhall, who every year vicariously *lives* the annual running of the greatest race on earth—the Iditarod, eagerly following the moment-by-moment news reports as to where each of his favorite dog teams is on the Iditarod Trail between Anchorage and Nome. Not anymore! Now I've got the bug too.

Just two weeks ago yesterday, I stood at the edge of the Broadway Melodies Theater, center stage for Royal Caribbean's wondrously beautiful *Rhapsody of the Seas,* during our third Alaskan cruise, and shared the story of Seppala, Togo, and the Great Serum Run with them. The audience was fascinated by the story. One young couple—possibly honeymooners, since they were ensconced in each other's arms—in the second row, were so captivated by the story I could tell they were *living* it. In retrospect, I wish I could retell it to them, now that this epiphany has cast its otherworldly glow on it. Permit me to explain what I mean: some years ago, when we were living on the banks of Maryland's beautiful Severn River, I happened to notice something unprecedented in my life happening. In that late afternoon sun a wooden planter filled with flowers was slowly accumulating an otherworldly radiance. I rushed inside to grab my camera; just in time, I captured some of it on film. Then, as suddenly as it came, the radiance disappeared; it was just another afternoon. Just so, in my mind at least, this glowing story (tied to the ever-changing phenomenon that is Alaska) has Velcrolike fastened itself so tightly in my subconscious that a bomb couldn't dislodge it.

Another contributing factor to the epiphany was a visit Connie and I made (during that same cruise) to a summer dog kennel for huskies in the hills above Juneau. I don't know what I expected to see and experience, but it most certainly didn't mesh with the reality. As our minibus approached its destination, it seemed like all the dogs in the world were barking at once! Well, one hundred fifty huskies barking full-torque at once—suffice it to say, it's an unforgettable experience. Until that moment, the dog-factor of sled-dog racing was just an abstraction in my mind. Suddenly, this collective howlerama blew years of misperceptions of what sled dogs were out of my mind, leaving me with a *tabula rasa* on which I might construct a new template.

For it didn't take long before I realized what all the howling was about. Just outside the circle of howling dogs (each one tied to a blue wooden hutch) was the beginning of a sled-dog team. And each of the unchosen one hundred fifty dogs was belting out a canine plea, *Hey there! Don't you dare leave me out! Don't you even think of not taking me along!* Every last one of them harbored an all-consuming dream: to pull a sled at full speed somewhere. Had any of the one hundred fifty ever raced in the Iditarod, undoubtedly they were now dreaming of doing it again.

We were permitted to look at, and pet, those huskies (most with Seppala Siberian ancestry in them) as we walked down the line. All the while, other huskies were being untethered from their hutches and brought over to the growing team. Believe me, each of those dogs was more than a handful! For the excitement over being chosen was so great they could hardly keep all four feet on the ground for the very rapture of what might lie ahead.

Who knows what goes through the mind of a wannabe sled dog? For starters, we must realize that since their life expectancy is only one-sixth of ours (that they're old by twelve), it means they have to cram into their moment-by-moment living six times as much intensity as we do.

At any rate, it took several dog handlers to keep them from tackling each other. Continually, they were messing up the lines attaching them to the tugline. And they'd leap high in the air in exuberant ecstasy at being among the elect. Just imagine trying to keep two dozen roughhousing little boys from tearing up a house—multiply that energy by at least six, and you have some idea of what it would be like to be a musher. Keep in mind that all this time the continual howls of outrage at being left behind from all the other dogs added up to an inimitable sound track. One that will remain in the archives of our minds forever.

At the end of this tugline was a cart large enough to carry up to a dozen people (total weight: a ton and a half). A wheeled cart because, though there was still snow on the slopes above, it had already melted down below. Someday I hope to be able to ride on a sled in snow. But mushers, in order to keep their sled dogs in year-round condition, yoke them to wheeled carts during the off-season months. And we tourists represent a serendipity: plenty of weight to pull (even more than normal, after getting off a cruise ship)!

Finally—after what must have seemed an eternity to the fourteen dogs, it was time to move out. As we did, so excited were the long-tied-up dogs that the musher had to keep the brake on to keep them from running away with us. We became acquainted with the commands: "Gee" for right, and "Haw" for left; "Mush! Hike! All right! Let's go!" all used to start the team; "Come Gee! Come Haw!" 180-degree turns; "Line out" command to lead team straight out from sled. I'd always thought that dog-sled speed was orchestrated by the musher; now I discovered that the lead dog would determine that, by maintaining steady pull, for if he or she slackens up, that demoralizes the dogs behind. And each dog behind the lead dog pulls equally hard. The end result, for a musher with a well-trained team, is to let the dogs do all the work; all the while trying to keep the team from exhausting their energy too soon.

All too soon, we heard the command to "Come Gee!" then "Come Haw!" as we made a 180-degree turn. Then the dogs were permitted to stop and rest in a long pool of water (refreshing to the dogs since they don't have sweat glands, but compensate through the pads of their feet and their lolling tongues). Since they overheat so easily (because of their two heavy coats), they relish stopping in cool water they may lap up. Then it was back in motion again, and all too soon our ride was at an end. Clearly, to the dogs, it was not nearly long enough.

I learned a lot more about sled dogs from Jeff Schultz's *Dogs of the Iditarod*. For starters, that the mushing life is all-consuming—anything but just a "day job." According to four-time Iditarod champion and professional dog musher Susan Butcher, "While most everyone has pets, these dogs are my workmates, friends, and family. I'm there when they're born and there when they die. If I succeed, it is because of them, and yet they are completely dependent on me. Until my marriage and having children, I'd never had a relationship with the intensity of bonding I've had with dogs during the Iditarod. There wasn't a year when I wasn't blown away by their capabilities and desire to go, even after a thousand miles" (Schultz, 8).

Iditarod veteran Judy Currier concurs: "These dogs are really our best friends.

We spend more time with them than we do with family, friends, or even each other" (Schultz, 10, 11).

Schultz notes that, in his many interviews with mushers, he has discovered that only dog lovers can understand the special bonding between mushers and their dogs; indeed, mushers love their dogs as intensely as parents love their children. "[Mushers] typically call out to their dogs in baby talk [it is said that the minds of adult dogs equate with two-year-old children, but that is not true of exceptional dogs] as a parent would talk to a newborn. Mushers will take their special dogs off their leads or out of their harnesses and let them run free, even in the mushers' homes" (Schultz, 11).

So what is it that mushers look for in their top dogs? First and foremost: a good head, a good coat, and a good constitution. Translated: "A *good head* means the dog has a happy attitude, a desire to travel, willingness to pull, and a love of running and running some more." One reason the Siberian bloodline is so central to mushers is that they are so honest; they don't play tricks on you, nor are they disloyal (Schultz, 23).

A *good coat* is also essential. During extreme cold and blizzards, when resting, dogs curl up with their backs to the wind, placing their tails over their noses to conserve heat and keep the nose from freezing.

As for a *good constitution,* four-time Iditarod mushing champion Martin Buser declares, "I look for athleticism in a dog. . . . Typically a good, fast dog has a narrow body and runs in a single, narrow track. It also has a deep chest to accommodate the requisite large lung capacity. It also means they must have good feet and be an eager eater and drinker." Five-time Iditarod champion Rick Swenson notes that "good feet don't snowball easily and the pads don't get cut easily." Some dogs are so tough you can look at their feet at the finish line, and after 1,200 miles they look as good as the day they started (Schultz, 25).

Training starts early. After pups are born, the mushers don't wait but are playing with them from the very first or second day to get them used to human contact. During weeks five to twelve, the pups are weaned and usually put into a large pen with litter mates and other pups—this socializes the dogs and cuts down on fighting. Mushers cannot tolerate unruly dogs. Mushers also early on take pups out for "puppy walks," usually accompanied by an adult dog or two. The pups remain in a large pen until they are four to six months old, when they each get their own doghouse. At six to nine months, they are "harness broken," usually by hooking them up with older, slower, retired lead dogs. According to four-time Iditarod mushing champion Doug Swingley, "Within the first hundred yards, they realize they are sled dogs and love it from then on."

As for Iditarod dogs, they normally run as rookies on slower noncompetitive teams when they are eighteen months to two years old. From these rookies, the musher looks for dogs (such as Togo) who early on evidence a fierce desire to be a lead sled dog. Those who prove themselves will race from the time they're two or three until they are old (twelve to as old as fourteen) (Schultz, 30–38).

Summing up the breed, Iditarod champion Joe Runyan says, "The sled dog, of which the Alaskan [h]usky is king, is not a breed of dog but, rather, a concept. The concept is 'pull hard and run fast!' . . . The sled dog is an ever-changing breed, always has been, always will be, and, hands down, the Alaskan [h]usky is the fastest and hardest-working dog alive." Doug Swingley agrees: "The Alaskan husky is the ultimate dog athlete. It is the decathlete of the dog world. The Alaskan husky can run faster, jump higher, and, if it could skip, skip better than any other dog alive. No dog in the world can do what the Alaskan husky can do" (Schultz, 41).

About this collection

This is our first ever collection of stories about the Far North (Norway, Alaska, British Columbia, Saskatchewan, Quebec, Newfoundland, Labrador, Arctic Circle). The animals featured include sled dogs, wolves, weasels, martens, rabbits, porcupines, lynxes, wolverines, bears (black, brown, polar), reindeer, eagles, and birds of many kinds—a veritable Who's Who of the North.

Other than Samuel Scoville Jr. and William Gerald Chapman, all the other writers will be new to readers of this animal series.

If you have not previously been acquainted with animals of the North, we think you will find them fascinating; if you already are, welcome to old friends.

CODA

I look forward to hearing from you! I always welcome the stories, responses, and suggestions that are sent to us from our readers. I am putting together collections centered on other genres as well. You may reach me by writing to:

Joe L. Wheeler, PhD
P.O. Box 1246
Conifer, CO 80433

* * * * *

STRANGE ENCOUNTER ON COHO CREEK

Morris Homer Irwin

The great Alaskan timber wolf was caught in a trap. But the trapper was dead—so the wolf would die there. And with her, her pups waiting in a nearby den. Could anything on earth save them?

* * * * *

One spring morning many years ago, I had been prospecting for gold along Coho Creek on southeastern Alaska's Kupreanof Island, and as I emerged from a forest of spruce and hemlock, I froze in my tracks. No more than twenty paces away in the flat muskeg was a huge, black Alaskan timber wolf—caught in one of Trapper George's traps.

Old George had died the previous week of a heart attack, so the wolf was lucky I had happened along. Yet now, confused and frightened at my approach, the wolf backed away, straining at the trap chain. Then I noticed something else: it was a female, and her teats were full of milk. Somewhere, there was a den of hungry pups waiting for their mother.

From her appearance, I guessed that she had been trapped only a few days. That meant her pups were probably still alive, surely no more than a few miles away. But I suspected that if I tried to release the wolf, she would turn aggressive and try to tear me to pieces.

So I decided to search for her pups instead and began to look for incoming tracks that might lead me to her den. Fortunately, there were still a few remaining patches of snow. After several moments, I spotted paw marks on a trail skirting the muskeg.

The tracks led a half-mile through the forest, then up a rock-strewn slope. I finally spotted the den at the base of an enormous spruce. There wasn't a sound inside. Wolf pups are shy and cautious, and I didn't have much hope of luring them outside. But I had to try. So I began imitating the high-pitched squeak of a mother wolf calling her young. No response.

A few moments later, after I tried another call, four tiny pups appeared. They couldn't have been more than a few weeks old. I extended my hands, and they tentatively suckled at my fingers. Perhaps hunger had helped overcome their natural fear. Then, one by one, I placed them in a burlap bag and headed back down the slope.

When the mother wolf spotted me, she stood erect. Possibly picking up the scent of her young, she let out a high-pitched, plaintive whine. I released the pups, and they raced to her. Within seconds, they were slurping at her belly.

What next? I wondered. The mother wolf was clearly suffering. Yet each time I moved in her direction, a menacing growl rumbled in her throat. With her young to protect, she was becoming belligerent. *She needs nourishment,* I thought. *I have to find her something to eat.*

I hiked toward Coho Creek and spotted the leg of a winter-killed deer sticking out of a snowbank. I cut off a hind quarter, then returned the remains to nature's icebox. Toting the venison haunch back to the wolf, I whispered in a soothing tone, "OK, mother, your dinner is served. But only if you stop growling at me. C'mon now. Easy." I tossed chunks of venison in her direction. She sniffed them, then gobbled them up.

Cutting hemlock boughs, I fashioned a rough shelter for myself and was soon asleep. At dawn I was awakened by four fluffy bundles of fur sniffing at my face and hands. I glanced toward the agitated mother wolf. *If I could only win her confidence,* I thought. It was her only hope.

Over the next few days, I divided my time between prospecting and trying to win the wolf's trust. I talked gently with her, threw her more venison, and played with the pups. Little by little, I kept edging closer—though I was careful to remain beyond the length of her chain. The big animal never took her dark eyes off me. "Come on, mother," I pleaded. "You want to go back to your friends on the mountain. Relax."

At dusk on the fifth day, I delivered her daily fare of venison. "Here's dinner," I said softly as I approached. "C'mon, girl. Nothing to be afraid of." Suddenly, the pups came bounding to me. At least I had *their* trust. But I was beginning to lose hope of ever winning over the mother. Then I thought I saw a slight wagging of her tail. I moved within the length of her chain.

She remained motionless. My heart in my mouth, I sat down eight feet from her. One snap of her huge jaws and she could break my arm . . . or my neck. I wrapped my blanket around me and slowly settled onto the cold ground. It was a long time before I fell asleep.

I awoke at dawn, stirred by the sound of the pups nursing. Gently, I leaned over and petted them. The mother wolf stiffened. "Good morning, friends," I said tentatively. Then I slowly placed my hand on the wolf's injured leg. She flinched, but made no threatening move. *This can't be happening,* I thought, *yet it is.*

I could see that the trap's steel jaws had imprisoned only two toes. They were swollen and lacerated, but she wouldn't lose the paw—if I could free her.

"OK," I said. "Just a little longer and we'll have you out of there."

I applied pressure; the trap sprang open, and the wolf pulled free. Whimpering, she loped about, favoring the injured paw. My experiences in the wild suggest the wolf would now gather her pups and vanish into the woods. But cautiously, she crept toward me.

The pups nipped playfully at their mother as she stopped at my elbow. Slowly, she sniffed my hands and arms. The wolf began licking my fingers. I was astonished. This went against everything I'd ever heard about timber wolves. Yet, strangely, it all seemed so natural.

After a while, with her pups scurrying around her, the mother wolf was ready to leave and began to limp off toward the forest. Then she turned back to me. "You want me to come with you, girl?" I asked. Curious, I packed my gear and set off.

Following Coho Creek for a few miles, we ascended Kupreanof Mountain until we reached an alpine meadow. There, lurking in a forested perimeter, was a wolf pack—I counted nine adults and, judging by their playful antics, four nearly full-grown pups. After a few minutes of greeting, the pack broke into howling. It was an eerie sound, ranging from low wails to high-pitched yodeling.

At dark, I set up camp. By the light of my fire and a glistening moon, I could see furtive wolf shapes dodging in and out of the shadows, eyes shining. I had no fear. They were merely curious. So was I.

I awoke at first light. It was time to leave the wolf to her pack. She watched as I assembled my gear and started walking across the meadow. Reaching the far side, I looked back. The mother and her pups were sitting where I had left them, watching me. I don't know why, but I waved. At the same time, the mother wolf sent a long, mournful howl into the crisp air.

* * * * *

Four years later, after serving in World War II, I returned to Coho Creek in the fall of 1945. After the horrors of the war, it was good to be back among the soaring spruce and breathing the familiar, bracing air of the Alaskan bush. Then I saw, hanging in a red cedar where I had placed it four years before, the now-rusted steel trap that had ensnared the mother wolf. The sight of it gave me a strange feeling, and something made me climb Kupreanof Mountain to the meadow where I had last seen her. There, standing on a lofty ledge, I gave out a long, low wolf call—something I had done many times before.

An echo came back across the distance. Again I called. And again the echo reverberated, this time followed by a wolf call from a ridge about a half-mile away.

Then, far off, I saw a dark shape moving slowly in my direction. As it crossed the meadow, I could see it was a black timber wolf. A chill spread through my whole body. I knew at once that familiar shape, even after four years. "Hello, old girl," I called gently. The wolf edged closer, ears erect, body tense, and stopped a few yards off, her bushy tail wagged slightly.

Moments later, the wolf was gone. I left Kupreanof Island a short time after that, and I never saw the animal again. But the memory she left with me—vividly, haunting, a little eerie—will always be there, a reminder that there are things in nature that exist outside the laws and understanding of man.

During that brief instant in time, this injured animal and I had somehow penetrated each other's worlds, bridging barriers that were never meant to be bridged. There is no explaining experiences like this. We can only accept them and—because they're tinged with an air of mystery and strangeness—perhaps treasure them all the more.

* * * * *

"Strange Encounter on Coho Creek," by Morris Homer Irwin. If anyone can provide knowledge of the earliest publication of this old story, the author, or the author's next of kin, please send to Joe Wheeler (P. O. Box 1246, Conifer, CO 80433). Morris Homer Irwin wrote around the mid-twentieth century.

The Baby and the Bear

Charles G. D. Roberts

Who could have even imagined such a thing! A raft at the mercy of a flooded river, and on the swirling raft: two babies—one a little child and the other a little bear cub. What was going to happen to them?

* * * * *

A stiffish breeze was blowing over Silverwater. Close inshore, where the Child was fishing, the water was fairly calm, just sufficiently ruffled to keep the trout from distinguishing too clearly that small, intent figure at the edge of the raft. But out in the middle of the lake, the little whitecaps were chasing each other boisterously.

The raft was a tiny one, four logs pinned together with two lengths of spruce pole. It was made for just the use to which the Child was now putting it. A raft was so much more convenient than a boat or a canoe, when the water was still and one had to make long, delicate casts in order to drop one's fly along the edges of the lily pads. But the Child was not making long, delicate casts. On such a day as this, the somewhat simple trout of Silverwater demanded no subtleties. They were hungry, and they were feeding close inshore; and the Child was having great sport. The fish were not large, but they were clean, trim-jawed, bright fellows, some of them not far short of the half-pound; and the only flaw in the Child's exultation was that Uncle Andy was not on hand to see his triumph. To be sure,

the proof would be in the pan that night, browned in savory cornmeal after the fashion of the New Brunswick backwoods. But the Child had in him the making of a true sportsman; and for him a trout had just one brief moment of unmatchable perfection—the moment when it was taken off the hook and held up to be gloated over or coveted.

The raft had been anchored, carelessly enough, by running an inner corner lightly aground. The Child's weight, slight as it was, on the outer end, together with his occasional ecstatic, though silent, hoppings up and down, had little by little sufficed to slip the haphazard mooring. This the Child was far too absorbed to notice.

All at once, having just slipped a nice half-pounder onto the forked stick which served him instead of a fishing-basket, he noticed that the wooded point which had been shutting off his view on the right seemed to have politely drawn back. His heart jumped into his throat. He turned, and there were twenty yards or so of clear water between the raft and the shore. The raft was gently, but none too slowly, gliding out toward the tumbling whitecaps.

Always methodical, the Child laid his rod and his string of fish carefully down on the logs, and then stood for a second or two quite rigid. This was one of those dreadful things which, as he knew, *did* happen, sometimes, to other people, so that he might read about it. But that it should actually happen to *him*! Why, it was as if he had been reading some terrible adventure, and suddenly found himself thrust, trembling, into the midst of it. All at once those whitecaps out in the lake seemed to be turning dreadful eyes his way, and clamoring for *him*! He opened his mouth and gave two piercing shrieks, which cut the air like saws.

"What's the matter?" shouted an anxious voice from among the trees.

It was the voice of Uncle Andy. He had returned sooner than he was expected. And instantly the Child's terror vanished. He knew that everything would be all right in just no time.

"I'm afloat. Bill's raft's carrying me away!" he replied, in an injured voice.

"Oh!" said Uncle Andy, emerging from the trees and taking in the situation. "You *are* afloat, aren't you! I was afraid, from the noise you made, that you were sinking. Keep your hair on, and I'll be with you in five seconds. And we'll see what Bill's raft has to say for itself after such extraordinary behavior."

Putting the canoe into the water, he thrust out, overtook the raft in a dozen strokes of his paddle, and proceeded to tow it back to the shore in disgrace.

"What on earth did you make those dreadful noises for," demanded Uncle Andy, "instead of simply calling for me, or Bill, to come and get you?"

"You see, Uncle Andy," answered the Child, after some consideration, "I was in a hurry, rather, and I thought you or Bill might be in a hurry, too, if I made a noise like that, instead of just calling."

"Well, I believe," said Uncle Andy, seating himself on the bank and getting out his pipe, "that at last the unexpected has happened. I believe, in other words, that you are right. I once knew of a couple of youngsters who might have saved themselves and their parents a lot of trouble if they could have made some such sound as you did, at the right time. But they couldn't, or, at least, they didn't; and, therefore, things happened, which I'll tell you about if you like."

The Child carefully laid his string of fish in a cool place under some leaves, and then came and sat on the grass at his uncle's feet to listen.

"They were an odd pair of youngsters," began Uncle Andy, and paused to get his pipe going.

"They were a curious pair, and they eyed each other curiously. One was about five years old, and the other about five months. One was all pink and white and ruddy tan and fluffy gold; and the other all glossy black. One, in fact, was a baby; and the other was a bear.

"Neither had come voluntarily into this strange fellowship; and it would have been hard to say which of the pair regarded the other with most suspicion. The bear, to be sure, at five months old, was more grown up, more self-sufficing and efficient, than the baby at five years; but he had the disadvantage of feeling himself an intruder. He had come to the raft quite uninvited and found the baby in possession! On that account, of course, he rather expected the baby to show her white, little teeth, and snarl at him, and try to drive him off into the water. In that case, he would have resisted desperately, because he was in mortal fear of the boiling, seething flood. But he was very uneasy, and kept up a whimpering that was intended to be conciliatory; for though the baby was small and by no means ferocious, he regarded her as the possessor of the raft, and it was an axiom of the wilds that very small and harmless-looking creatures might become dangerous when resisting an invasion of their rights.

"The baby, on the other hand, was momentarily expecting that the bear would come over and bite her. Why else, if not from some such sinister motive, had he come aboard her raft, when he had been traveling on a perfectly good tree? The tree looked so much more interesting than her bare raft, on which she had been voyaging for over an hour, and of which she was now heartily tired. To be sure, the bear was not much bigger than her own Teddy bear at home, which she was wont to carry around by one leg, or to slap without ceremony whenever she thought it needed discipline. But the glossy black of the stranger was quite unlike the mild and grubby whiteness of her Teddy, and his shrewd, little, twinkling eyes were quite unlike the bland shoe buttons which adorned the face of her uncomplaining pet. She wondered when her mother would come and relieve the strain of the situation.

"All at once, the raft, which had hitherto voyaged with a discreet deliberation, seemed to become agitated. Boiling upthrusts of the current, caused by some hidden unevenness in the bottom, shouldered it horridly from beneath, threatening to tear it apart; and unbridled eddies twisted it this way and that with sickening lurches. The tree was torn from it and snatched off reluctant all by itself, rolling over and over in a fashion that must have made the cub rejoice to think that he had quitted a refuge so unreliable in its behavior. As a matter of fact, the flood was now sweeping the raft over what was, at ordinary times, a series of low falls, a succession of saw-toothed ledges that would have ripped the raft to bits. Now the ledges were buried deep under the immense volume of the freshet. But they were not to be ignored, for all that. And they made their submerged presence felt in a turmoil that became more and more terrifying to the two little passengers on the raft.

"There was just one point in the raft, one only, that was farther away than any other part from those dreadful, seething, crested, black surges, and that was the very center. The little bear backed toward it, whimpering and shivering, from his corner.

"From her corner, directly opposite, the baby, too, backed toward it, hitching herself along and eying the waves in the silence of her terror. They arrived at the same instant. Each was conscious of something alive, and warm, and soft, and comfortable, with motherly suggestion in the contact. The baby turned, with a sob, and flung her arms about the bear. The bear, snuggling his narrow, black snout under her arm, as if to shut out the fearful sight of the waves, made futile efforts to crawl into a lap that was many sizes too small to accommodate him.

"In some ten minutes more, the wild ledges were past. The surges sank to foaming swirls, and the raft once more journeyed smoothly. The two little voyagers, recovering from their ecstasy of fear, looked at each other in surprise; and the bear, slipping off the baby's lap, squatted on his furry haunches and eyed her with a sort of guilty apprehension.

"Here it was that the baby showed herself of the dominant breed. The bear was still uneasy and afraid of her. But she, for her part, had no more dread of him whatever. Through all her panic, she had been dimly conscious that he had been in the attitude of seeking her protection. Now she was quite ready to give it, quite ready to take possession of him, in fact, as really a sort of glorified Teddy bear come to life; and she felt her authority complete. Half coaxingly, but quite firmly, and with a note of command in her little voice which the animal instinctively understood, she said, 'Tum here, Teddy!' and pulled him back unceremoniously to her lap. The bear, with the influence of her comforting warmth still strong upon him, yielded. It was nice, when one was frightened and had lost one's mother, to be cuddled so softly by a creature that was evidently friendly in spite of the dreaded man-smell that hung about her. His mother had tried to teach him that that smell was the most dangerous of all the warning smells his nostrils could encounter. But the lesson had been most imperfectly learned, and now was easily forgotten. He was tired, moreover, and wanted to go to sleep. So he snuggled his glossy, roguish face down into the baby's lap and shut his eyes. And the baby, filled with delight over such a novel and interesting plaything, shook her yellow hair down over his black fur and crooned to him a soft babble of endearment.

"The swollen flood was comparatively quiet now, rolling full and turbid over the drowned lands, and gleaming sullenly under a blaze of sun. The bear having gone to sleep, the baby presently followed his example, her rosy face falling forward into his woodsy-smelling black fur. At last the raft, catching in the trees of a submerged islet, came softly to a stop, so softly as not to awaken the little pair of sleepers.

"In the meantime, two distraught mothers, quite beside themselves with fear and grief, were hurrying down stream in search of the runaway raft and its burden.

"The mother of the baby, when she saw the flood sweeping the raft away, was for some moments perilously near to flinging herself in after it. Then her backwoods common sense came to the rescue. She reflected, in time, that she could not swim, while the raft, on the other hand, could and did, and would carry her treasure safely enough for a while. Wading waist-deep through the drowned fields behind the house, she gained the uplands, and rushed, dripping, along the ridge to the next farm, where, as she knew, a boat was kept. This farmhouse, perched on a bluff, was safe from all floods; and the farmer was at home, congratulating himself. Before he quite knew what was happening, he found himself being dragged to the boat—for his neighbor was an energetic woman whom few in the settlement presumed to argue with, and it was plain to him now that she was laboring under an unwonted excitement. It was not until he was in the boat, with the oars in his hands, that he gathered clearly what had happened. Then, however, he bent to the oars with a will which convinced even that frantic and vehement mother that nothing better could be demanded of him. Dodging logs and wrecks and uprooted trees, the boat went surging down the flood, while the woman sat stiffly erect in the stern, her face white, her eyes staring far ahead.

"The other mother had the deeper and more immediate cause for anguish. Coming to the bank where she had left her cub in the tree, she found the bank caved in, and tree and cub together vanished. Unlike the baby's mother, she *could* swim; but she knew that she could run faster and farther. In stoic silence, but with a look of piteous anxiety in her eyes, she started on a gallop down the half-drowned shores, clambering through the heaps of debris, and swimming the deep, still inlets where the flood had backed up into the valleys of the tributary brooks.

"At last, with laboring lungs and pounding heart, she came out upon a low, bare bluff overlooking the flood, and saw, not a hundred yards out, the raft with its two little passengers asleep. She saw her cub, lying curled up with his head in the baby's arms, his black fur mixed with the baby's yellow locks. Her first thought was that he was dead—that the baby had killed him and was carrying him off. With a roar of pain and vengeful fury, she rushed down the bluff and hurled herself into the water.

"Not till then did she notice that a boat was approaching the raft, a boat with two human beings in it. It was very much nearer the raft than she was, and traveling very much faster than she could swim. Her savage heart went near to bursting with rage and fear. She knew those beings in the boat could have but one object, the slaughter, or, at least, the theft, of her little one. She swam frantically, her great muscles heaving as she shouldered the waves apart. But in that race she was hopelessly beaten from the first.

"The boat reached the raft, bumped hard upon it, and the baby's mother leaped out, while the man, with his boat hook, held the two craft close together.

The woman, thrusting the cub angrily aside, clutched the baby to her breast, sobbing over her, and threatening to punish her when she got her home for giving so much trouble. The baby did not seem in the least disturbed by these threats, to which the man in the boat was listening with a grin, but when her mother started to carry her to the boat, she reached out her arms rebelliously for the cub.

" 'Won't go wivout my Teddy bear,' she announced, with tearful decision.

" 'Ye'd better git a move on, Mrs. Murdoch,' admonished the man in the boat. 'Here's the old b'ar comin' after her young'un, an' I've a notion she ain't exactly ca'm.'

"The woman hesitated. She was willing enough to indulge the baby's whim, the more so as she felt in her heart that it was in some respects her fault that the raft had got away. She measured the distance to that formidable black head, cleaving the water some thirty yards away.

" 'Well,' said she, 'we may as well take the little varmint along, if Baby wants him.' And she stepped over to pick up the now shrinking and anxious cub.

" 'You quit that, an' git into the boat, quick!' ordered the man, in a voice of curt authority. The woman whipped round and stared at him in amazement. She was accustomed to having people defer to her; and Jim Simmons, in particular, she had always considered such a mild-mannered man.

" 'Git in!' reiterated the man, in a voice that she found herself obeying in spite of herself.

" 'D' ye want to see Baby et up afore yo'r eyes?' he continued sternly, hiding a grin beneath the sandy droop of his big mustache. And with the baby kicking and wailing and stretching out her arms to the all-unheeding cub, he rowed rapidly away, just as the old bear dragged herself up on the raft.

"Then Mrs. Murdoch's wrath found words, and she let it flow forth while the man listened as indifferently as if it had been the whistling of the wind. At last she stopped.

" 'Anything more to say, ma'am?' he asked politely.

"Mrs. Murdoch answered with a curt 'No.'

" 'Then all *I* hev' to say,' he went on, 'is, that to *my* mind *mothers* has *rights*. That there b'ar 's a mother, an' she's got feelin's, like you, an' she's come after her young un, like you—an' I wasn't a-goin' to see her robbed of him.' "

* * * * *

"The Baby and the Bear," by Charles G. D. Roberts. Published in St. Nicholas, *April 1913. Original text owned by Joe Wheeler. Charles G. D. Roberts wrote stories about wildlife for popular magazines during the first few decades of the twentieth century.*

HEROES OF THE FAR NORTH

C. L. Paddock

A storm—indeed a blizzard—was upon them. What a welcome sight: a lighted cabin window.
But what was inside blanched the face of Verner Johnson.
Impossible!
But how could he say no?

* * * * *

Verner Johnson and his dog, Prince, seemed to be the center of attraction in the great throng that had gathered far north of the United States boundary, at Prince Albert, Saskatchewan, on the occasion of the opening of Prince Albert National Park. The premier of Canada, Right Honorable W. L. Mackenzie King, and other men of influence, were there, but they were rather pushed in the background by these heroes of the North—Johnson and Prince.

On a large elevated platform, beautifully decorated with pine boughs and the Union Jack, stood a man of slight yet sturdy build, with open face bronzed by wind and sun, and with eyes of keenest blue, and near him sat his great powerful husky, Prince.

From his looks and his actions, it was plain to see that Johnson was out of his element. He is a man of shrinking disposition, one who seeks not the plaudits and acclamations of men. Out on the trail with his dogs, he bravely faced the snow and the cold and the blizzard, but there on the flag-draped platform, with his dog and the prime minister, and surrounded by thousands of people, he did not feel at home. It was evident that he was nervous, for his left hand closed and unclosed around the flag-draped rail, in an effort to steady his trembling limbs, while his right hand grasped tightly the collar of his dog. Prince showed his unconcern by yawning in the face of the prime minister. These proceedings meant nothing to him.

As they stood there in the gaze of the throng, the premier presented Mr. Johnson with a certificate of the Royal Humane Society for saving the life of Miss Rose Littlewood. "To the innate chivalry of valorous men, such as you, Mr. Johnson," said the premier, "who perform deeds of service and of courage, without hope of reward, is due much of the glamour that brightens the pages of the history of our country. It is my pleasure and my honor to present to you this certificate, which represents as high an honor as can be bestowed upon you. It is a written acknowledgment of your brave and splendid character, and with it goes the highest praise of your fellow men."

"Shucks," said Johnson, when the ceremony was all over, "there was no sense in that thing this afternoon. I didn't do anything any ordinary man wouldn't have done. And anyway, Prince did the big part of the job." But it was a risk which most men would not have taken. They would have excused themselves by saying it was none of their affairs.

But you want to know the story of this man of the Far North, whose life, or much of it, had been spent back from the haunts of men, in the wilds. The only way of reaching the isolated sections of the Far North in winter is by dog train, and Johnson has made numerous trips through deep snow and in the face of high winds, when the thermometer registered many degrees below zero.

It was in January of 1928 that Johnson and his faithful dogs were mushing along through the woods, headed north. The day was dark and sullen, and the sky was overcast. There was a stillness that precedes the storm—only the *crunch, crunch, crunch* of the snow beneath his feet and the padding of his dogs ahead of him could be heard. It was an ominous silence. Johnson urged his team to greater speed, for he felt sure a blizzard was soon to break, and he was certain, too, that a cabin was not far in the distance, where they could find shelter. Ordinarily the sun is visible only a few hours each day in winter, but on this day there had been no sun, and night was settling down even earlier than usual. Soon all was darkness, but ahead on the shore was to be seen a glimmer of light from the cabin. Johnson knew that welcome and warmth awaited him there, for while he would find no luxuries in this home, more than one hundred twenty miles from the nearest railroad station, what is one man's is every man's in the Northland.

Johnson didn't even stop to knock. The custom of the country did not demand it. Unharnessing his faithful dogs, he threw each of them a fish and entered the cabin. The greeting he received was unexpected. Another visitor was there, an unwelcome guest, more unwelcome because of the surroundings. The shadow of death was hovering over that humble dwelling.

The owner of the cabin was absent, and there was no way of telling when he would return. On a rude bed lay a young girl, just barely conscious. All day her frail body had been racked with pain, which had grown worse as the hours wore away. A woman was moving about, doing all that she knew how to do. Anxiety was written on her tired face, for she felt sure the girl had appendicitis; and it was plain to be seen that if medical attention could not be had at once, it would be too late. There was a sled outside the door, but the dogs had gone with the father. Should she load the suffering girl on a sled and attempt to pull her the hundred twenty miles through the snow and the storm to the nearest railroad station? A blizzard was threatening, and she knew what a blizzard meant. It might last an hour, and it might last a day or a week. It was while she was debating just what would be best to do that Johnson entered, snow covered and well-nigh exhausted.

The rising winds already whistled through the pines, and the snow was being driven in clouds by the wintry blasts. But the groans of a human being in need gripped Johnson's heart, and with no thought of what his decision might mean to him, he said, "I'll take her down." He busied himself reharnessing his already tired dogs while the woman wrapped the girl in warm furs and blankets. In half an hour they were started on their long journey to the railway.

When eight miles had been covered, the runner of the sleigh broke, and the brave driver must return to the cabin. Most men would have been discouraged, but not Johnson. You and I can never realize what those eight miles meant to him. He stayed just long enough to change sleighs, and then once more plunged out into the storm in the dead of night. The blinding blizzard had covered the trail, but he urged his dogs on, trying almost in vain to keep them in the beaten track. The blizzard blew the snow into his clothes, where it melted and ran in chilly streams down his body, finally freezing his garments into sheaths of ice. He could scarcely breathe. His eyeballs were inflamed by the blinding snow. But on and on they went, ten, twenty, thirty miles. Finally he realized he was lost, and they were traveling in circles. What should he do? He wondered if the girl was alive or dead, but he dared not look. He must go on.

However, there is a limit to human endurance. His long day trip, coupled with this harrowing night journey, had sapped his strength and slowed up his movements. In order to keep going, he held on to the handles of the sleigh, now and then jumping on the runners to ride for a short rest.

There was only one chance—to depend on Prince, the lead dog, the finest in all Saskatchewan, and champion of the famous derby. But they were facing death, and although it was one chance in a million, they *must take that once chance.* Perhaps Prince's eyes could see what his could not, and he would find the way through the stormy, trackless wastes of snow.

"Mush, mush on, Prince," he called, and the dogs and the sleigh were in motion again.

Hoping against hope, Johnson followed blindly, trusting brave Prince to lead them into haven. He says he knows little of what happened after that, perhaps little more than the unconscious girl.

Just at dawn he saw a mile in the distance a few scattered cabins, and his courage revived. It was a village—Big River—the farthest north settlement on the Canadian National Railroad in Saskatchewan. Prince had won.

As fortune would have it, a freight train was standing at the station, waiting for the blizzard to subside. When Johnson had told his story, the train was canceled, and the engine and caboose were ordered to make a hurried run of one hundred sixty miles to Prince Albert with the unconscious girl.

Then followed one of the wildest runs ever made on that part of the Canadian National System. Everything on the division was ordered onto sidings that the locomotive, in its race with death, might have the right of way. At Prince Albert, one hundred sixty miles away, an ambulance and surgeons were in waiting. In the hospital, nurses made the operating room ready. At last, with the sound of escaping steam, the engine came to a stop, the precious freight it carried was hurried to the hospital, and the operation was performed. "One hour more," said the surgeon, "and it would have been hopeless."

While the locomotive was making its record run to Prince Albert, Johnson, up in Big River, too tired to seek shelter in some friendly home, sagged to the floor of the tiny railway station, and slept with a clear conscience and the satisfaction of having been a help to one in need. Prince burrowed into the soft snow outside, and he, too, slept with a sense of duty well done. They had raced with death, and won. "Greater love hath no man than this, that a man lay down his life for his friends."

* * * * *

"Heroes of the Far North," by C. L. Paddock. Published in Youth's Instructor, *vol. 77, no. 12. Published by permission of Joe Wheeler (P.O. Box 1246, Conifer, CO 80433) and Review and Herald Publishing, Hagerstown, MD 21740. C. L. Paddock wrote nature-related stories during the first half of the twentieth century.*

THE BLACK CAT

Samuel Scoville Jr.

The pine marten is the swiftest tree climber in the world—bar one. Unfortunately for the marten, that one exception had seen him. And once the black cat (also known as fisher and pekan) sees prey, it is all but over.

So the race was on.

* * * * *

Above the afterglow gleamed a patch of beryl green. Etched against the color was the faintest, finest, and newest of crescent moons. It almost seemed as if a puff of wind would blow it, like a cobweb, out of the sky. As the shifting tints deepened into the unvarying peacock blue of a northern night, the evening star flared like a lamp hung low in the west. The dark strode across the shadows of the forest, which lay cobalt blue against the drifted snow. As the winter stars flamed out, a tide of night life flowed and throbbed under the silent trees. One by one the wild folk came forth to live and love and die in this their day, even as we humans in ours. On the edge of the woods the white-footed mice crept up the dry weed stalks from their tunnels beneath the snow, and frolicked and feasted on the store of seeds scattered and piled by the wind in every cranny of the vast whiteness. Their backs were the color of dry pine needles, and they wore silky, snowy waistcoats and stockings. Sniffing blindly, a fierce fragment of flesh and blood, with a

CHARLES LIVINGSTON BULL

muzzle like a tiny tapir and a crooked crocodile jaw filled with keen teeth, rushed with amazing swiftness toward a nearby group of feasting mice. Covered with gray, plushy fur, the strange head of the beastling showed no signs of eyes or ears. Although far larger, the mice scattered before him as man would before the rush of a tiger, for it is the doom of the blarina shrew that every twenty-four hours he must eat thrice his own weight in flesh and blood. Tonight, before he had time to single out from the scattering group his victim, a dark, soft shadow flapped across the snow like some gigantic moth. It hung for a moment over the scurrying little throng—and fell. When it lifted, the shrew was gone. In the starlight the snow told the story. At the end of the burrowing, tunnel-like trail of the blarina was stamped in the snow a great X, which is the sign and seal of the owl folk, just as a K is the signature of the hawk people. There the trail of the blarina stopped, while a tiny spot of blood put a period to the last snow story that the blarina would ever write. From a treetop beyond, sounded the dreadful voice of the great horned owl.

Long after the twilight had dimmed into a jeweled darkness, opalescent with the changing colors of the northern lights, from the inner depths of the woods there came a threat to the life of nearly every one of the forest folk. Yet it seemed but the mournful wail of a little child. Only to the moose, the black bear, and the wolverine was it other than the very voice of death.

Fifty feet above the ground, from a blasted and hollow white pine, the mournful call again shuddered down the wind. From a hollow under an overhanging bough, a brownish-black animal moved slowly down the tree trunk headfirst, which position of itself marked him as a past master among the tree folk. Only those climbers who are absolutely at home aloft go forward down a perpendicular tree trunk. As the beast came out of the shadow, it resembled nothing so much as a big black cat with a bushy tail and a round, grayish head. Because of this appearance, the trappers have named it the black cat. Others call it the fisher, although it never fishes, while to the Indians it is the pekan—the killer-in-the-dark. In spite of its rounded head and mild, doggy face, the fisher belongs to those killers, the weasels.

On reaching the ground, the pekan followed one of the many runways that he had discovered in the ten-mile beat which made up his hunting ground. Like most of the weasels, he lived alone. His brief and dangerous family life lasted but a few days in the autumn of every year. When his mate tried to kill him unawares, the black cat knew that his honeymoon was over and departed back again to his own hollow tree, many miles away from Mrs. Black Cat. Tonight, as he moved leisurely across the snow in a series of easy bounds, his lithe black body looped itself along like a hunting snake, while his broad forehead gave him an innocent, open look. If in the tree he had resembled a cat, on the ground he looked more like a dog.

There was one animal who was not misled by the frank openness of the fisher's face. That one was a hunting pine marten, who had just come across a red squirrel's nest made of woven sticks, thatched with leaves, and set in the fork of a moose-wood sapling some thirty feet from the ground. Cocking his head on one side, the marten regarded the swaying nest critically out of his bright black eyes. Convinced that it was occupied, with a dart he dashed up the slender trunk, which bent and shook under his rush. Chickaree, however, had craftily chosen a tree that would bend under the lightest weight and signal the approach of any unwelcome visitor. Before the marten had covered half the distance, four squirrels boiled out of the nest, and, darting out to the farthest twigs, leaped to the nearest trees and scurried off into the darkness. The marten had poised himself for a spring when he saw the fisher gazing up at him, and straightway forgot that there were squirrels in the world. With a tremendous bound he landed on the trunk of a nearby hemlock and slipped around it like a shadow.

It was too late. With effortless speed the black cat reached the trunk and slipped up it like a black snake. The marten doubled and twisted and turned on his trail, and launched himself surely and swiftly from dizzy heights at arrowy speed. Yet spring and dash and double as he would, there was always a pattering rush just behind him. Before the branches, which crackled and bent under the lithe, golden-brown body, had stopped waving, they would crash and sag under the black weight of the fisher. With every easy bound, the black came nearer to the gold. The pine marten is the swiftest tree climber in the world—bar one. The black cat is that one. As the two great weasels flashed through the trees, they seemed to be running tandem. Every twist and turn of the golden leader was followed automatically by the black wheeler, as if the two were connected by an invisible, but unbreakable, bond.

Under the strain it was the nerves of the marten that gave way first. Not that he stopped and cowered helpless and shaking like the rabbit folk, or ran frothing and amuck, as do rat kind when too hardly pressed. No weasel, while he lives, ever loses his head completely. Only now the marten ran more and more wildly, relying on straight speed and overlooking many a chance for a puzzling double which would have given him a breathing space. The imperturbable black cat noted this, and began to take shortcuts that might have lost him his prey at the beginning of the chase.

At last the long and circling chase brought them toward a vast white pine that towered forty feet away from the nearest tree. A bent spruce leaned out toward the lone tree. With a flying leap, the marten reached the spruce and flashed up the trunk with never a look behind. His crafty pursuer saw his chance. Landing in a broad crotch of the spruce, with a flying takeoff he launched himself outward and downward into midair with every ounce and atom of spring that his steel-wire muscles held. It seemed impossible that anything without wings could cover the great gap between the two trees, but the black cat knew to an inch what he could do, and almost to an inch did the distance tax his powers. In a wide parabola, his black body whizzed through the air half a hundred feet above the ground, beginning as a round ball of fur which stretched out until the fisher hung full length at the crest of his spring. If the tree had been a scant six inches farther away, the black cat would never have made it. As it was, the huge, clutching, horn-colored claws of his forepaws just caught and held long enough to allow him to clamp down his hold with his hind paws. The marten, who had started fifty feet ahead of the black cat and had lost his distance by having to climb up, jump, and then climb down, passed along the trunk of the pine on his way to the ground, his lead cut down to a scant ten feet. Without a pause, the pekan deliberately sprang out into the air and disappeared in a snowbank full forty feet below.

Not many animals, even with a snow buffer, could stand a drop of that distance, but the great black weasel burst out of the snow, his steel-bound frame apparently unjarred, and stood at the foot of the tree. As the marten reached the ground and saw what was awaiting him, his playful face seemed to turn into a mask of rage and despair. The round black eyes flamed red; the lips curved back from the sharp teeth in a horrible grin; and with a shrieking snarl and a lightning-like snap, he tried for the favorite throat hold of the weasel folk. He was battling, however, with one quite as quick and immeasurably more powerful. With a little bob, the black cat slipped the lead of his adversary, and the flashing teeth of the marten closed only on the loose, tough skin of the fisher's shoulder. Before he could strike again, the black cat had the smaller animal clutched in its fierce claws with no play to parry the counter thrust of the black muzzle, which in another second had a death grip on the golden throat. Throughout the whole fight and the blood-stained finish, the black cat's face was the mild, reflective face of a gentle dog.

With a single flirt of its black head, the fisher flung the limp body of the marten over its shoulder, and, winding its way up the tree trunk, cached it for the time in a convenient crotch, feeling sure that no prowler would meddle with a prey which bore upon its pelt the scent and seal of the black cat.

All through the two-day snowstorm the fisher had kept to its tree, and its first kill of the night had only sharpened its appetite. Following the nearest runway, it came to the shore of a wide, rapid, little forest river, which at this point had a fall that insured current enough to keep it from freezing. Near its bank the ranging black cat came upon a fresh track in the soft snow. First there were five marks, one small, two large, and two small. The next track showed only four marks, with the order reversed, the larger marks being in front instead of behind the smaller. A little way farther, and the smaller marks, instead of being side by side, showed one behind the other.

The black cat read this snow riddle at a glance. The five marks showed where a northern hare, or snowshoe rabbit, had been sitting, the fifth mark being where its bobbed tail had touched the snow. The larger marks had been the marks of the fur snowshoes that it wears in winter on its big, hopping, hind legs, and the smaller, the mark of the little fore paws which, when sitting naturally, touched the ground in front of the hind paws. When the hare hopped, the position was reversed, as the big hind paws with every hop struck the ground in front of the others, the hare traveling in the direction of the larger marks. The last tracks showed that the hare had either scented or seen its pursuer, for the hare's eyes are so placed that it can see either frontward or backward as it hops. As the little fore legs touched the ground, they were twisted one behind another, so as to secure the greatest leverage possible. The black cat settled doggedly down to the chase. Although far slower in a straightaway run than either the hare or the fox, it can and will run down either in a long chase, although it may take a day to do it.

Tonight the chase came to a sudden and unexpected end. The hare described a great circle, nearly half a mile in diameter, at full speed, and then, whiter than the snow itself, squatted down to watch his back trail and determine whether his pursuer was really intending to follow him to a finish. Before long the squatting hare saw a black form on the other side of the circle, with humped back looping its way along.

At such a sight the smaller cottontail rabbit would have run but a short distance and then crouched in the snow, squealing in fear of its approaching death. The hare is made of sterner stuff. Moreover, this one was a patriarch fully seven years old, a great age for any hare to have accomplished in a world full of foes. Wabasso, as Hiawatha named him, had not attained to these years without encountering black cats. In some unknown way, probably by a happy accident, he had learned the one defense that a hare may interpose to the attack of a fisher and live. Reaching full speed almost immediately, he cleared the snow in ten-foot bounds, four to the second, while the wide, hairy snowshoes that nature fits to his white feet every winter, kept him from sinking much below the surface.

Although the same color as the snow, the keen eyes of the black cat caught sight of the hare's movement, and he at once cut across the diameter of the circle. In spite of this shortcut, the hare reached the bank of the open river many yards ahead. Well out in the midst of the rushing icy water lay a sandbar, now covered by snow. To the black cat's amazement and disgust, and contrary to every tradition of the chase, this unconventional hare plunged with a desperate bound fully ten feet out into the icy water. Wabasso was no swimmer and had evidently elected to travel by water in the same way that he had found successful by land. Kicking mightily with his hind legs, he hopped his way through the water, raising himself bodily at every kick, only to sink back until but the top of his white nose showed. Nevertheless, in a wonderfully short time he had won his way through the wan water and lay panting and safe on the sandbank. If pursued, he could take to the water again and hop his way to either shore, along which he could run and take to the water whenever it was necessary.

Tonight no such tactics were needed. The fisher, in spite of his name, hates water. He can swim, albeit slowly and clumsily, in summertime. As for leaping into a raging torrent of ice-cold water—it was not to be considered. The black cat raced up and down the bank furiously, and not until convinced that the rabbit was on that snowbank for the night did he give up the hunt and go bounding along the bank of the river after other and easier prey. For the first time that night the mildness of his face was marred by a snarling curl of the lips, showing the full set of cruel, fighting teeth with which every weasel, large or small, is equipped.

As the black cat followed the line of the river, his sharp ear caught a steady, monotonous sound, like some one using a peculiarly dull saw. Around a bend the still water was frozen. Against the side of the bank an empty pork keg had drifted down from some lumberman's camp and frozen into the ice. In front of the shattered keg crouched a large, blackish, hairy animal, gnawing as if paid by the hour. It was none other than the Canada porcupine, Old Man Quill-pig, as he is called by the lumberjacks, who hate him because he gnaws to sawdust every scrap of wood that has ever touched salt. The porcupine saw the black cat, but never ceased gnawing. Many and many an animal has thought that he would kill sluggish, stupid quill-pig. The wolf, the lynx, the panther, and the wildcat all have tried—and died. So tonight the porcupine kept on with his sawing under the starshine, convinced that no animal that lived could solve his defense. The black cat, however, is one of two animals which have no fear of the quill-pig. Black bear is the other. With its swift, sinuous gait, the pekan came closer, whereupon the quill-pig unwillingly stopped his sawing and thrust his head under the broken, frozen staves of the barrel. His body hugged the ground, and in an instant he seemed to swell to double his natural size, as he erected his quills and lashed this way and that with his spiked tail. Pure white, with dark tips, the quills were thickly barbed down to the extreme point, which was smooth and keen. These barbs are envenomed, and wherever they touch living flesh, cause it to rankle, swell, and fester—for all save the pekan. Tonight the black cat wasted no time. Disregarding the bristling quills and lashing tail, the crafty weasel suddenly inserted a quick paw underneath the gnawer, and, with a tremendous jerk, tipped him over on his bristling back. Before the quill-pig could right himself, the fisher had its teeth in the unprotected underparts, and the fight was over. Throughout the struggle, the black cat disregarded the porcupine's quills entirely. Many of them pierced his skin. Others were swallowed as the victor feasted on his prey. By reason of some unknown charm, the barbed quills can do no harm to a black cat.

As the pekan ate and ate, the stars began to dim in the blue-black sky, and a faint flush in the east announced the ending of his hunting day. With a farewell mouthful, he started back through the snow for his hollow tree, making a long detour to bring in the cached marten. As he approached the tree from whose crotch the slim golden body had dangled, his leisurely lope changed into a series of swift bounds. For the first time a snarl came from back of the pekan's mild mask. The dead marten was gone from the tree. In an open space, which the wind had swept nearly clear of snow, it lay under the huge paws of a shadowy gray animal with luminous, pale-yellow eyes, a curious bob of a tail, and black-tufted ears. For all the world it looked like a gray cat, but such a cat as never lived in a house. Three feet long and forty pounds in weight, the Canada lynx, among the cats of this continent, is surpassed in size only by that huge yellow cat, the puma or panther. At the snarl of the fisher, the cat looked up, and, at the sight of the gliding black figure, gave a low, spitting growl and contemptuously dropped his great head again to the dead marten.

For a moment the big black weasel and the big gray cat faced each other. At first sight it did not seem possible that the smaller animal would attack the larger, or that, if he did, he could last long. The fisher was less than half the size and weight of the lynx, who also outwardly seemed to have more of a fighting disposition. The tufted, alert ears, the eyes gleaming like green fire, and the bristling hair and arched back contrasted formidably with the broad forehead and round, honest face of the fisher.

So, at least, it seemed to young Jim Linklater, who, with his uncle Dave, the trapper, lay crouched close in a hemlock copse. Long before daylight the two had traveled on silent snowshoes up the riverbank, laying a trapline, carrying nothing but a backload of steel traps. At the rasping growl of the lynx, they peered out of their covert, to find themselves not thirty feet away from the little arena.

"That old lucifee'll rip that poor little black innocent to pieces in jig-time," whispered Jim.

Old Dave shook his grizzled head. He pulled his nephew's ample ear firmly and painfully close to his mouth. "Son," he hissed, "you and that lucifee are both goin' to have the surprise of your lives."

Unwitting of his audience, the weasel approached the cat swiftly. Suddenly, with a hoarse screech, the lynx sprang, hoping to land with all his weight on the humped-up black back and then to bring into play his ripping curved claws while he sank his teeth deep into his opponent's spine.

It was at once evident that lynx tactics have not yet been adapted for black cat service. Without a sound the pekan swerved like a shadow to one side, and the lynx had scarcely touched the ground before the fisher's fierce, cutting teeth had severed the tendon of a hind leg, while his curved claws slashed deep into the soft inner flank. The great cat screeched with rage and pain and sheer astonishment. As he landed, the crippled leg bent under him. Even yet he had one advantage which no amount of courage or speed on the part of the pekan could have overcome. If only the lynx had gripped the dead marten and sprung out into the deep snow, the fisher must have had to fight a losing fight. Like the hare, the lynx is shod with snowshoes in the winter, on which he can pad along on snow in which a fisher would have sunk deep at every step.

In spite of his formidable appearance, however, the lynx has a plentiful lack both of brains and courage. As his leg doubled under his weight, in a panic he threw himself on his back, the traditional cat attitude of defense, ready to bring into action all four of his sets of sharp tearing claws, with his teeth in reserve. Against another of the cat tribe, such a defense would have been good. Against the pekan it was fatal. No battler in the world is a better in-fighter than the black cat, and any antagonist near his size who invites a clinch rarely comes out of it alive.

The pekan first circled the spinning, yowling, slashing lynx more and more rapidly, until there came a time when the side of the gray throat lay before him for a second unguarded. It was enough. With a pounce like the stroke of a coiled rattler, the pekan sprang, and a double set of the most effective fighting teeth known among mammals met deep in the lynx's throat. With all of his sharp eviscerating claws, the great cat raked his opponent. The black cat, however, protected by his thick pelt and tough muscles, was content to exchange any number of surface slashes for the throat hold. Deeper and deeper the crooked teeth dug until they pierced the jugular vein itself. The struggles of the lynx became weaker and weaker, until, with a last convulsive shudder, the gray body stretched out stark in the snow.

It was young Jim who first broke the silence.

"Those pelts'll bring all of twenty-five dollars," he remarked, stepping forward.

"Help yourself," suggested old Dave, not stirring however from where he stood.

At the voices, the black weasel sprang up like a flash. With one paw on the dead lynx and another on the marten, he faced the two men in absolute silence. Suddenly the eyes under the mild forehead flamed red and horrible, and the dripping body quivered for another throat hold.

"Seems like Mr. Black cat wants 'em both," observed the old man, discreetly withdrawing from the farther side of the copse.

Jim gazed into the flaming eyes a moment longer and then followed his uncle. "He ain't so blame innocent, after all," he murmured.

* * * * *

"The Black Cat," by Samuel Scoville Jr. Published in St. Nicholas, *September 1919. Original text owned by Joe Wheeler. Samuel Scoville Jr. wrote nature stories for popular magazines during the first half of the twentieth century.*

HIS THIRD ENEMY

Hubert Evans

The boy was determined to land the great rainbow trout. But then a fierce bald eagle entered the contest.
So who would win: the boy, the eagle, or the trout?

* * * * *

The willows crowding the pool's low banks had once more put on June's sprightly garb of green. Farther upstream, the wing beats of a male willow-grouse sounded like the roll of a primitive drum celebrating spring's return. From sheltered bays of the lake, a mile away, came the gossiping, lazy honks of feeding wild geese. And on the big spruce overlooking the pool, a bald-headed eagle launched its jubilant whistle.

For the eagle the lean forage of winter was but a memory, and now that the pool was free of ice, it kept sharp watch on this favorite fishing ground. Many a luscious trout had it lifted from that pool. Again it whistled, as if in response to the unsettling, throbbing urge of awakening life that every wild thing in that northland valley seemed to sense.

Even Flash, the great rainbow trout, had responded to the stirring summons of the spring and had returned to summer feeding grounds. All winter he had lain in the gloom under the tangle of the old beaver dam at the foot of the pool. Ten

feet below the dark ceiling of ice he had rested, with slowly fanning fins, not moving from his lair, indifferent to food. Now he was ravenous.

At the head of the pool, where the hard-driven water surged over boulders, he rose boldly. So large, so superbly strong was he that after every rush, the ripples spread even to the calm waters of the pool. The talons of the eagle shifted slightly on its branch, and as Flash's broad tail left a second boiling eddy, the bird gathered itself for a lightning swoop.

A good five pounds did Flash, this giant of Willow Creek, weigh. His back was superbly rounded, his flanks hard and clean. In all that unspoiled British Columbia valley, there were few to equal him in perfection of form, in strength, or in fighting spirit. Others of his kind might desert their mountain streams for the rich forage of the lake, but for him the fast water held an allure, a challenge, not to be found in the easy living of the lake. On the clean gravel of a riffle a short distance upstream he had been hatched, and here he had remained. Now, in his seventh spring, he was the pool's undisputed overlord, and until that June morning, no human eye had found him.

The eagle had seen the stranger, but so slowly and noiselessly had the young sportsman come that neither Flash nor any of the lesser trout were aware of him. He stood now knee-deep in the shallows at the head of the pool, keeping well within the fringe of shade cast by the willows, so that his shadow would not fall upon the water. With growing excitement the youth saw the great fish break water a second time. The big eagle watched hungrily, not daring to swoop, yet determined not to desert his prize.

The water swirled around the young angler's firmly planted legs while he stood watching the pool with that mixture of delight and caution that comes to every true angler when he finds himself within striking distance of the fish of his dreams. Then with great care he withdrew to the bank and began setting up his rod.

Experienced fly fisherman though he was, the youth's fingers trembled a little as he untied the tapes of his rod case.

"He's the daddy of 'em all," he whispered, grinning at the excitement his voice betrayed.

When he had set up the rod, he threaded the smooth casting line through the guides, knotted a moist leader to it, and brought his fly box from the pocket of his worn fishing coat.

March Brown, large dressing, would be as good as any, he mused. *Still, the light's strong; better not try too large a fly,* he decided, changing the March Brown for one a size smaller.

When he had threaded the gut through the eyed hook, he began edging toward the water. Without entering it, he faced obliquely downstream and began switching the slender, six-ounce rod back and forth above his head, at the same time running out line from the reel with his left hand. A preparatory cast well to the left of the feeding trout showed him he had a good thirty feet of line out. This was enough to reach the spot of the last rise.

Elbow well into his side, he brought the rod smartly to a vertical position, paused while the line straightened behind him, then steadily, unhurriedly, brought it forward until it paralleled the surface. The line rolled out; gently as a snowflake the fly struck the surface and settled as smoothly as if it had been dissolved. Drawing in a foot or two of slack line, he looped it lightly in his left hand and twitched the rod tip provocatively as it slowly lifted.

But since that rise, Flash had moved two yards upstream. A foot above the bottom he lay, poised and ready, easily holding himself head-on to the swift current. He did not see the fly. His bluish back, with its sprinkling of round black spots, and his silver sides, each marked with its lateral line of red, made him almost invisible against the white and gray mosaic of the pebbles. The surging rise and fall of the fast water threw grotesque, moving patterns of shadow across him. And then, straight ahead and above, he saw the fly as it was falling to the surface a second time.

The fly never struck the water. With unbelievable speed Flash shot upward, hurled himself clear, and seized it while it was still above the surface. The pure silver flashed as all the morning sunlight seemed to focus on his underparts. Then he went under, leaving a foaming swirl. Not until he swung his head into the current again did the mighty rainbow suspect the unnaturalness of the fly.

Even then he did not guess its full menace. He shook his head to get clear of the slight but steady strain of the line. It seemed to yield, but as he swerved into faster water, the maddening pull increased, and he knew he had been tricked. With vicious suddenness the battle began.

Swinging about, then, Flash charged down the pool. Above him the taut line tore a foaming rent in the smooth fabric of the surface. He shot out toward the barrier of the old beaver dam. Close to it, he hesitated for a split second to feel if he had shaken free from his invisible enemy. But the young angler twitched his bowed rod sharply, increasing the strain. Then it was that the big trout began those tactics which have earned the rainbow of the Pacific slope the reputation of being among the world's gamiest and most spectacular fighting fish.

Doubling back on the line, he headed for the top of the pool. Then cutting sharply upward, Flash hurled himself into a curving leap. Two yards on, he smote the water again and seemed actually to bounce upward, this second time going a good three feet into the air. A third leap followed instantly and then, diving, he kept close to the bottom as he shot into the fast water again.

The speed and strength of his weaving tactics were irresistible. The angler on the bank was still frantically recovering the slack line when Flash, close to the bottom now, raced parallel to the far bank. There were no swerves this time, for he was headed for his lair below the overhang of the old dam. Under and up through the tangle of old cuttings he shot; the line fouled, the leader came taut with a savage jerk, the hook pulled loose!

On the bank, seventy feet away, the youth reeled in the limp line. Before he saw the broken leader, he knew the trout had outwitted him, and he knew it would be futile to fish the pool again that day. Setting down his rod he studied the pool, observing the nature of every underwater hazzard, in readiness for the combat he was planning—the combat when he, and not the trout, would be the victor.

I'll make my cast from the far bank next time, he thought. *Keep a bit upstream from that tangle under the dam, where I can give him the butt good and plenty if he tries that trick again. Man alive! What a scrapper he is!* And then, fishermanlike, his thoughts turned to the coming fight and to the time when he would take the great trout in triumph to the distant ranch house.

It seemed like sacrilege to fish for lesser trout that day, so he took down his rod and climbed the low bank. *I'll wait two days,* he thought as he looked back at the pool. *Then I'm coming for my revenge, old-timer.*

But as he set off down the dim trail toward home, he did not know how strange his next—and last—meeting with Flash would be. Nor could Flash, sulking in his lair, know that the pool he had ruled so long was soon to betray him to his enemies. The man vanished, and soon the eagle's sinister shadow skimmed the surface as this second enemy returned to its lookout.

The big rainbow did not leave his lurking place until the long northland twilight was falling. The shadows of the willows had grown long across the pool and had melted into the spreading dusk before he swam slowly to the feeding place below the boulders. There, until day surrendered completely to encroaching night, he fed, warily at first, then hurled himself confidently at the stone-fly larvae the water bore down to him. When full night came, he was gorged and indifferent to food.

Sometimes Flash might lie in the narrow eddies at the pool's upper end until the filtering gray of dawn heralded the morning feeding time. But tonight, by that undefined sense that warns most fish of an approaching storm, Flash sensed the rain already falling in the mountains to the northwest. He turned and swam indolently to his lair. There, ten feet below the surface, he was lying under the overhang of rotting sticks when the first big drops began to fall.

These first drops came with a measured deliberateness, each pricking the surface sharply and raising a bubble that gyrated slowly in the gloom. Suddenly the tiny dome of each became alive with brightness as a lightning flash stabbed the night. Thunder, the voice of his third and most treacherous enemy, went grumbling away among the hills; and then, as if this had been a signal to assault, the rain torrent came pounding down.

When tardy dawn came at last, Willow Creek was rising rapidly. The full violence of the deluge had struck in the mountains where the stream had its source. For miles along its bank, depressions in the forest floor brimmed with water and overflowed in a thousand feeding rivulets into the creek.

When Flash moved uneasily from the gloom of his lair, he swam through an unbroken cloud of silt. Particles of rotten leaves, root fiber, spruce needles, and moss mingled with the earth stain in the swirling water. The sensitive nerves along his flanks caught the dull pounding of falling water, where the stream took the descent over the decaying beaver dam. Flash moved to a narrow back eddy behind a stone, moody, vaguely uneasy because of some danger not yet defined.

As he lay in the cramped refuge behind the stone, he became aware of an abrupt change in the current's direction. He was swinging to meet it head-on when the water—even the banks of the stream—seemed to tremble sickeningly, and then the thousands of tons of pent-up water charged him in a solid wall. The old beaver dam, unrepaired for years, had burst!

Pebbles, waterlogged sticks, even the stone behind which Flash had taken shelter, all began to move, drawn across the bottom by the terrific suction of the widening break. Flash, caught broadside, was rolled half over. He lurched, dodged, strove mightily to keep from being swept away.

Through the silt fog, the smaller trout zigzagged to right and left, searching in terror for a hiding place. But among the moving debris of the bottom there was none to be found. Only Flash was strong enough to fight the full sweep of wild water and win. A few lesser trout found safety under the curving bank. The rest were swept away, some to be choked with debris and buried in the leaves and branches that littered the overflowing banks.

Not until late that afternoon, when the sun shone again through the clearing water, did Flash realize how alarmingly his domain had changed. There were no deep holes now, no varied currents and backwaters. Instead, the water fell vertically over the boulders and ran in a shallow, swift canal between new banks scoured through what had been the bottom of the wide pool. The channel was nowhere more than ten feet wide, and nowhere could the great trout find more than a foot of water to cover him. In growing alarm he retreated to where the dam had been. But now the current was divided, frayed into foam by the tangle of sticks. He was trapped and at the mercy of his enemies.

Next morning, at sunrise, the eagle returned to its fishing lookout on the spruce. The water of Willow Creek was clear again, and from his point of vantage the keen eyes of the feathered fisherman could mark every trout in the raw channel below. It spread its powerful wings, hopped from the branch, and swooped. Its shadow swept like a black menace over the surface and Flash, warned, but powerless to gain deeper water, shot downstream as if seeking the lost safety of his lair. The eagle banked steeply and dropped for him.

In a desperate effort to escape, Flash charged the tangle of sticks, but it was like a net cunningly spread to capture him. The water frothed between the old branches, but there was no space for him to pass through. With a mighty effort he floundered about; his spread tail found purchase against the sticks, and he threw himself clear just as the eagle, with talons outthrust, dropped for him.

Back up the channel the big trout raced, leaving a following wake that betrayed his course to the enemy. The eagle glided in pursuit. It knew now that the great trout was its prize, that the shallows offered him no cover, and that only pursuit was needed to capture him.

As the eagle glided closer to its quarry, one of the smaller trout, thrown into panic by the moving shadow, shot away, found itself in shallower water, and in trying to turn back, stranded itself among the stones. Its striving tail was drenching the pebbles when the eagle shot down and bore it, writhing vainly, to the top of the spruce tree.

Half an hour later the gliding shadow was over the water again. This time Flash shot upstream to the falls. But the plunging water, striking a ledge of hardpan that the freshet had exposed, proved as treacherous as the ruined dam. His broad tail sent the water spouting behind him as he sped away.

Hardly was he clear of the falls when the eagle plunged. Its talons grazed the trout's back, but Flash, dodging, got clear. The eagle rose heavily. To left and right, up and down, Flash darted, but the feathered pursuer, not to be shaken off, kept behind, craftily following as the trout came closer and closer to the barrier of sticks. When they were twenty feet from it the eagle made a feint, and Flash, cornered now, shot squarely at the network.

For just a second the eagle hovered, its great wings beating the air. It was in the very act of diving to seize the struggling trout when it caught signs of movement in the willows of the near bank. Zooming steeply to view the intruder clearly, it saw the young angler. But it did not surrender by flying away.

Dumbfounded, the fisherman plunged clear of the brush and stared at the area of mud-caked stones where the pool had been only two days before. And the eagle, seeing Flash hopelessly fouled among the sticks, folded its wings and dropped like a plummet. Not until that fatal instant did the young angler from the ranch house see the great trout. With a shout he leaped to the end of the ruined dam, slipping and stumbling, and came along its crest, hoping to reach the breach in time.

But the eagle, with victory at hand, was not to be driven off so easily. Only a chance had saved Flash before, and now the eagle came on boldly. Its cruel, hooked beak sought for him among the smother of water and leaves that his thrashing tail threw up. The whole mat of sticks shook as the youth leaped down into the breach, and there was a scream of defiance as the eagle soared, circling angrily overhead.

The angler paid no heed to it. Here was the great trout that had outwitted him. No carefully planned attack was needed now. Flash, with straining gill-covers, lay panting at his feet, and the boy need only pick him up and bear him home in triumph.

But because he was a true angler and loyal to the ethics of his craft, he hesitated only a moment. Then stooping, he wet his hands, took hold of Flash and carefully slipped him over the tangled sticks and into the deep, fast-running water below. For a second or two the rainbow lay dazed, then with a sure sweep of his tail shot away, down toward deeper reaches of Willow Creek. The eagle, defeated, soared to its lookout, and the young angler, looking downstream, knew Flash would not stop until he gained the lake. The chances were that he and the mighty rainbow would never meet again and yet, because he was a sportsman, there was satisfaction in his eyes and a smile on his face, as he reviewed the thrilling events of the last few moments.

* * * * *

"His Third Enemy," by Hubert Evans. Published in St. Nicholas, *August 1930. Original text owned by Joe Wheeler. Hubert Evans wrote nature stories for popular magazines during the first half of the twentieth century.*

PATSY ANN
Queen of Juneau

Joseph Leininger Wheeler

Even today, two-thirds of a century after her passing, the people of Alaska's capital city remember her. After all, she—well, her sculptured likeness—still greets them at the wharf.

So what is it about this bull terrier that is so unforgettable? Let's find out.

* * * * *

Patsy Ann (a bull terrier) was born in Portland, Oregon, on October 12, 1929, just seventeen days before Black Tuesday, the stock market crash heard around the world. A purebred puppy, sent north by ship, she was intended for the twin daughters of a Juneau dentist. When that didn't work out, she moved in with the Dean Rice family—and when *that* didn't work out, she moved in with the one family that unreservedly loved her, the good citizens of Juneau.

Though deaf from birth, for some inexplicable reason, she was able to somehow "hear" the whistle of a ship—even from half a mile out.

Instinctively, she always knew at which dock a ship would tie to—contributing no little to her legend was the time when everyone was given what turned out to be erroneous information as to where a certain ship would dock. Puzzled, Patsy Ann gazed at the crowd for a long moment, then turned and trotted over to the correct dock.

Though no Juneau home was closed to her, she chose to hang out at the Long-shoremen's Hall, quite likely because the men there were as interested in ships' arrivals as she was. The men needed to know when and where a given ship would dock—and Patsy Ann needed to be needed.

Between ship dockings, she made the rounds of her faithful providers—which included every business in town. One particular fan could be counted on to slip her a candy bar every day—quite possibly a contributing factor to her increasing rotundity as she got older (as, alas! the complicity of ship cooks).

When the steamers anchored out in the harbor, Patsy Ann often swam out to pay her respects to the passengers. She would then perch on the ship's rudder until someone gave her a ride back to shore. When the tourist season was over for the year, she'd support the arts by wandering up and down the aisle at the Coliseum Theater during musical performances.

Old Juneau's Ambassador to the world in time became the most famous dog west of the Mississippi, more photographed even than Rin Tin Tin. During her reign during the 1930s and early 1940s, postcards depicting her were sold everywhere. She was even the subject of a book by local author Carl Burrows in 1939.

She had her title validated by the mayor himself; in 1934, Mayor Goldstein dubbed her "Official Greeter of Juneau, Alaska."

In 1934, when a city ordinance was passed requiring the registration of all dogs—not to worry: several citizens bought a license for her; they then presented her with a bright red collar. Which she politely wore—for a time, then disdainfully discarded it; clearly, the Queen was not amused.

Hundreds of thousands of tourists carried her fame with them when they left.

For most of her life, she'd head at a fast trot for the right dock whenever she sensed a ship was coming in. Not unlike her human counterparts, however, as she grew older that gait began to slow. Her rheumatic gait was also exacerbated by her unscheduled dives into the icy waters of the Gastineau Channel.

Fittingly, she quietly died on March 30, 1942, in the Longshoremen's Hall. The next day, at her city-wide funeral, her tiny little coffin was lowered into the Gastineau Channel.

Fifty years after her death, her statue (sculpted by New Mexico artist Anna Burke Harris) was commissioned by the "Friends of Patsy Ann" and installed on the wharf waterfront she knew so well. Clippings of dog hair sent in from all over the world were stirred into the bronze at the time of casting, symbolically uniting the spirits of dogs everywhere.

Thus it is that hundreds of thousands of tourists continue to be greeted by Patsy Ann. Next time you're in Juneau, be sure to pay your respects to her: touch and pet her, photograph her, and *remember* her.

* * * * *

"Patsy Ann: Queen of Juneau," by Joseph Leininger Wheeler. Copyright © 2010. Printed by permission of the author.

A RACE FOR AN UNKNOWN PRIZE

Roy J. Snell

The North has never been easy to survive in. Especially for Eskimo children in years past, with few food choices, especially during the long winter.
So Florence and her friends came up with a unique fund-raising plan.
But would the reindeer obey orders?

* * * * *

Chapter one

Florence Huyler was worried. Every moment the intensity of the arctic storm was increasing.

"Nowadluk!" she called to the girl who rode the sled ten feet ahead of her. "Nowadluk! Are we lost?"

There came no answer. Hunched up on her sled, gripping the reins, the Eskimo girl continued to look straight ahead. Florence's words had been blown away by the wind.

We are lost, the American girl told herself. *I am sure of it.*

It was disappointing, this wild storm on her first reindeer journey. She had meant it to be a real holiday. And now, here they were with night coming down upon them, a wild gale sweeping in from the arctic shores of Alaska, and no definite knowledge of their whereabouts. It had started out so joyously. Nowadluk's brother had driven the deer down from the deer camp forty miles away to Cape Prince of

Wales in Alaska, where Florence was helping her father with his mission work.

Nowadluk had said, "We may drive sled back if we wish. By-and-by come back with Okbaok and his dog team. Want to go?"

Did she! At first Florence's life at the Cape had been interesting and exciting. But with the nine-month-long winter settled down upon them, with letters coming by dog team only once a month, and the days growing shorter and shorter, she had begun to feel shut in.

There were many other reasons why she particularly wanted to take this trip; but she was not to think of these just now, for suddenly her reindeer wheeled sharply to the right and went speeding away into the gathering night.

"Whoa!" she screamed. "Whoa, Bouncer! Whoa!"

She may as well have called to the wind to cease blowing. Her lead dog, Ginger, would have understood her words, but not this wildly racing reindeer.

"Nowadluk!" she screamed. "Nowadluk!" Again the wind caught her words and blew them away. A moment more and she was not only lost but alone in a great white world of whirling snow.

At first she jerked on her line. Then—recalling that this was a sign to go faster—she allowed the line to hang slack, gripped the swaying sled, and calmly awaited the end.

The reindeer took one more sudden turn to the right. This time Florence's sled went over, and she rolled beneath it. Holding to the sled with all her strength, she went bumping along over the frozen ground. All the time she was striving in vain to push the heavy sled off her chest and to right it.

There came a sudden shock, another, and still another. Then she went rolling over and over while deer, sled, sleeping bag, and all disappeared into the gray shroud that is an arctic storm in the gathering night.

Struggling to her feet, she looked about her. The reindeer had completely disappeared. Back of her, so close that she could almost touch it, was a black, wall-like mass.

"Willows!" she exclaimed. "Willows with leaves on them. The leaves were caught by the frost and did not fall!"

This was better. Dressed in a reindeer parka, heavy corduroy slacks, and mukluks, with these willows as a windbreak and a fire burning before her—she could endure the night and the storm. But Nowadluk?

"Nowadluk!" she called.

To her waiting ears came only the sound of rushing wind and rustling leaves.

Crawling far back among the protecting leaves, she crouched low and listened. Five minutes passed, eight—ten. Slow business this—waiting for one knows not what.

Suddenly she pressed forward, listening intently. Had she heard the bark of a dog?

How impossible! The deer herder's camp must still be miles away. And yet—she stood up. She *had* heard something. This time it was a faint, distant "Who-whee!"

Cupping her hands, she screamed, "Who-whee!"

At last a black hulk appeared. It was Nowadluk.

"Where is your reindeer?" Florence exclaimed.

"Gone!" said the Eskimo girl. "All alike, these reindeer. No good." The Eskimo girl sighed.

"We'll make a fire. It will be great fun!"

"No!" said the practical native girl, who more than once had braved the chill of an arctic night. "Not fun, but we will do what you say. Perhaps tonight the wind stops. Then we find camp. We—"

She stopped and leaned forward to listen.

"Dog barks," she whispered.

"I thought I heard—"

"Reindeer," Nowadluk broke in.

What did it mean? The sharp, insistent bark of a dog sounded louder and louder. At the same time the sound of reindeers' hoofs told that they, too, were coming closer.

The girls were on their feet when two dark forms loomed up in the night. Just as Nowadluk sprang forward, these forms veered off to the right and began to fade away in the distance. Behind them, still barking sharply, raced a dog.

"Our reindeer!" Florence exclaimed.

"Yes."

"But the dog?" Florence was amazed. "If he catches them, will he kill them?"

"Not kill," said Nowadluk. "This dog is a reindeer dog. Perhaps not go far." She added, "Better follow."

All at once the *click, click* of the reindeers' hoofs ceased, and the quality of the dog's bark changed.

"Come!" exclaimed Nowadluk. "Very fast!"

Florence was strong, a true out-of-doors girl, but she was astonished at her native companion's speed and endurance. When at last the dark bulks—now standing quite still—once again appeared through the snow fog, Florence was all but exhausted.

To their joy, they discovered that those dark bulks were indeed their reindeer, that their sleds had become entangled in the willows, and that the well-roped packs were none the worse for their bumping journey.

As they came up, a beautiful golden collie raced forward to meet them.

"Good boy!" Florence exclaimed. She bent over to pat the glorious creature's head. "Whose is he?" she asked.

"Don't know," said Nowadluk. "Not belong to our reindeer camp. That one dog he belongs somewhere. Perhaps not too far. By-um-by he starts to go there. Then we follow."

True to her prediction, once he saw their sleds straightened up and reins prepared, the dog looked first at one then at the other. Then, like some human guide, he walked slowly away into the wild, windy night.

"Aren't dogs wonderful?" Florence asked.

The dog gave a low, joyous bark, then sprang away toward the light. A square of brighter light appeared against the gray sky, and a shrill voice called, "Here, Stardust! Here! Where are you?"

"A girl," Florence whispered. "Who is she?"

"I don't know," the native girl answered. The dog raced forward. The girls followed slowly.

Faye Mills, Stardust's owner, lived with her father at Shishmaref Island, thirty miles farther north. Part of their herd of reindeer belonged to a number of Eskimos. This was the time for counting, branding, and setting aside deer for the winter's food supply; so they were camped on the tundra. Her father had gone to the trading post for additional supplies.

"So you are here alone on the tundra?" said Florence, looking with keen approval upon the slim, dark-eyed girl who seemed about her age.

"Not alone." The girl smiled. "There is Stardust." She patted the golden collie. "He is a wonderful dog."

"Yes," Florence agreed. "He surely is. But he deserted you tonight."

"Only to bring me some good company." The girl's tone was full of good cheer. "I am often lonely. But you? You must have gotten lost!" she exclaimed. "And you must be starving! The stew is hot. The teakettle is steaming. I'll have tea in a jiffy. Then we'll talk."

After the meal was over they sat around the glowing stove and talked while the tent swayed in the wind.

"You know," said Florence, "I like Alaska. Fresh air, grand exercise, plenty of thrills and adventure, always something new. But"—her face grew sober— "our people need so much.

"Only last summer little Kudlucy, a perfectly adorable child, became ill. We took her to the doctor on the mail boat. He said, 'All she needs is light food, oatmeal, bread, canned milk. Not so much meat.' "

"I know," Faye sighed. "But how are they to get it? Father tells of selling reindeer at Nome and sharing the money with our Eskimos. We have taught them to use our food. Now there is little market for reindeer meat. Bowman Brothers at Nome supply all that, and our people—"

"Go hungry," said Florence. "But you know," she leaned forward eagerly, "I've been wondering if we couldn't do something to attract attention to our reindeer. Suppose we were to plan a reindeer race between herds—your herd, our herd, and the Bowmans' at Nome."

"How would that help?" Faye's brow wrinkled.

"You never can tell," was Florence's reply. "It would be sure to get into the papers in the States. We have a short-wave radio sending set. We'd get the news of the race out to Seattle. And we'd add something about the needs of our people. Anyway, we could try it. We—"

She stopped abruptly. In her enthusiasm she had plunged her hands into her sweater pockets. A paper crumpled under her hand.

"Oh! That letter!" she exclaimed in dismay. "I brought it with me.

"It's queer," she murmured, smoothing out a bit of paper. "This letter is addressed to Father and me by a perfect stranger. It says he's coming to the Cape, and he hopes we'll aid him in ascertaining certain facts. What facts? I wonder. He's due to arrive anytime. It is all so delightfully mysterious." Her voice trailed off.

"Yes," said Faye, "it is strange how people move in and out of our lives up here where the world begins."

For an hour longer they sat by the fire, planning a grand reindeer race. It would be a girls' race—Faye with an Eskimo girl as her companion, Florence and Nowadluk.

"And the Bowman twins at Nome!" exclaimed Faye. "They'll be strong for it. They are always hunting excitement. All Nome will welcome the idea. The winter is so long, and there's nothing to stir things up."

Three days the storm roared on. On the fourth day Florence and her companion headed for their own camp. After exchanging their reindeer for a dog team, they pushed straight on for home. Their friends would be worrying about the blizzard and their long stay.

It was night, with a glorious moon hanging overhead, when again they sighted the snowy cap of Cape Prince of Wales Mountain.

"Home again soon," Nowadluk said cheerfully.

She spoke too soon, for from the distance—out where the ice drifts toward the North Pole—there came a call for help.

"That," said the Eskimo girl, "is a white man. Ice is drifting from shore. We must help white man."

"A white man!" Florence exclaimed. "Who can it be? So few come this way! Oh!" her voice rose. "It must be the man of mystery who wrote that letter. I wonder—Nowadluk!" She gripped the Eskimo girl's arm. "Can he be in much danger?"

"Very bad!" said Nowadluk. "Wind off shore. Ice drifts. Between this man and shore broad, black water. Very bad!"

"We must try to get him off the ice floe." There was fear in the white girl's voice. "It is a long way to the Cape, and there is no one to help us. What can be done?"

Chapter two

"Nowadluk"—there was a huskiness in Florence's voice—"we must try to rescue that man. If we go to get help, it may be too late."

"Too bad," said Nowadluk. "Ice must be far from shore. Maybe hundred feet. But look!" she exclaimed, pointing away toward the sand dunes. "There is Azazruk's place. Gone to Nome, Azazruk. But his kayak, it is there. This white man on ice, he must use kayak. I go bring it. You find that man."

Once again there came that appeal for aid.

"Help! Help! Help!"

It sounded strange in the white silence of the arctic night.

"Coming!" Florence called. "We are coming!"

Ten minutes later she stood beside a band of inky water that lay between her and the drifting ice floes. But where was the man?

"Where are you?" she called.

"Here!" came the answer. "Farther north. The floe is drifting rapidly. If it gets into the Arctic and breaks up—"

The man did not finish, but the girl knew the rest. There was need for haste. If the ice floe broke up, the man would be lost.

At last she saw the man and his five dogs lined up before a towering ice pile. She shuddered as she watched a great, silent force moving them relentlessly northward. The distance across that black gulf was great, and it was slowly growing wider. How were they to save this man?

"My companion has gone for a kayak," Florence called across the water.

"A kayak?" the man questioned. "Oh, yes, that's some sort of native skin boat."

After that, for a quarter of an hour she followed along the solid ice, keeping an eye on the man and his dogs as they drifted steadily northward.

And then she began hearing welcome sounds. "Gee! Haw! Mush now!" It was Nowadluk.

"Ah-ne-ca! It is far!" the Eskimo girl exclaimed as she looked across the black waters. "Perhaps too far."

"What shall we do?"

Nowadluk made no answer. After lifting the light kayak off her sled, she groped around in its prow until she drew out a coil of leather rope. At the end of this was a block of wood the size of a man's fist. From this block protruded four sharp barbs. This block, Florence knew, was used by native hunters to recover game that had been shot some distance from shore. But how was Nowadluk to use it now?

Unlike her sisters, Nowadluk had practiced all manner of hunting tricks with her brother. She knew the art of throwing this retriever. But had she the strength and skill required for such a long throw?

Carefully she arranged the coil. Then, holding it lightly in her left hand and taking the block of wood in her right, she swung lightly on her toes, threw back her arm, and let go.

"Too bad!" she groaned, as the block fell a full twelve feet short of its mark.

"Try again!" There was a touch of despair in the white girl's voice.

Once again the missile sped on its way.

"A little better!" Florence encouraged. "Try once more!"

"Too bad—cannot do this!" Nowadluk groaned, sinking down on the ice.

"Look!" Florence exclaimed. "Over there is a free cake of ice. It comes out ten feet or more. Try there."

The man moved over to his right and stepped out on the loose cake of ice. It tilted a little, but he held his footing.

"Now!" The Eskimo girl breathed a prayer.

"Right at me!" the man encouraged.

Right at him it was, and this time right into his gloves.

Rapidly Nowadluk gave him his instructions. The rope was long. He was to pull the kayak across. She would keep enough rope to pull it back. He would load two dogs into the kayak. She would pull them across. After that two more dogs. And so in time man, dogs, and sled would be saved.

The man obeyed the native girl's instructions to the last detail. When two fine dogs reached the solid shore ice, Florence wanted to shout for joy; and when at last the man grasped her hand and was helped from the kayak, she did let out a triumphant shout.

"You girls performed wonders!" exclaimed the man. His voice was husky. "I shall not forget."

"But why were you on the ice floes?" Florence asked in a puzzled tone.

"That," said the stranger, laughing a trifle uncertainly, "is just what I don't know."

"You—you don't know?" Florence stared.

"I was headed for the Cape Prince of Wales Mission."

"Our mission," said Florence.

"I had guessed you were from the mission. Well," the man went on, "when I came to Cape Prince of Wales Mission, I had to go around it. I trusted my dogs to follow the trail. Apparently this is once they failed me, for after an hour I found myself on the drifting floes with no way to get back to shore. What could have happened?"

"Your dog team took the trail made by polar bear hunters," Florence explained. "They go hunting on the floes. Close to the Cape the ice often crowds the shore so closely that you do not know when you go upon it. That's what happened to you."

"And I hate to think what more might have happened," the man added with a shudder. "And now?"

"Now we head our dog teams toward a pot of coffee and a kettle of steaming Mulligan stew," Florence laughed.

* * * * *

Thirty days later the race was on—from Citnezok to Nome, many miles away.

Florence found herself riding behind Blixen—the largest, most powerful sled deer of their herd. Every nerve of the young girl was atingle.

A strange race it was! Before her, trotting after her own sled, was Nowadluk. The two of them, with their deer, made up a team. The contestants had been started one hour apart. Florence and Nowadluk had drawn first place. One hour behind her was Faye Mills and her Eskimo companion, and one hour behind them came the Bowman sisters. Whoever covered the ground in the shortest time would win.

Each reindeer drew a sled. The driver might ride or trot along behind, as she chose. At first, when the deer was fresh and traveled fast, Florence and Nowadluk had ridden. Now, as the deer began to tire, the girls trotted along over the hard-packed trail. The running time would be eight or ten hours. Days were short; it would be long after dark when they arrived.

Florence planned to get pictures of her rivals as they came in; with a candid camera and flash bulb arrangement in the pack on her sled, she was all prepared. These pictures would go out by airplane to Seattle. They would appear in every large daily paper in America. The interest in this, the first all-Alaska reindeer race, had surpassed all expectations. And yet, there had been moments of discouragement. As the winter wore on, more and more of the native children had fallen ill because of improper diet. Florence and her father had donated all they could from their meager supply of food, but it was not enough.

"Just what do you hope to gain by this race?" the man saved from the floes had asked one day.

"We are hoping something good will come of it," was all Florence could say.

This man had remained a person of mystery. His interest in reindeer appeared boundless. He had asked questions about them by the hour. He had even hired an Eskimo to drive him up to the Cape Prince of Wales and the one belonging to the Shishmaref Island people. Then one morning he thanked them for all their kindness, bade them a cheery goodbye, and headed back toward Nome.

"Got something up his sleeve," had been Mr. Huyler's comment.

As Florence thought all this through, her feet went *pop, pop, pop* on the hard-packed trail.

At Dave's Lodge, some twenty miles from their starting place, the girls learned the glad news that their time so far was better than that of the other teams. They were winning! But could they keep it up?

Suddenly, as they crossed a beach strewn with driftwood, Florence's reindeer trace caught on a snag. Her sled was thrown over. She went sprawling, and her deer fell with a rattle of antlers to the frozen earth. At once her heart was in her mouth. Was her reindeer seriously injured, her part in the race at an end?

The answer came quickly. Hardly had she untangled the drawstrap than the deer was on his feet again and flashing away. But time had been lost. At the next lodge she was told that all racers were running neck-and-neck.

At the point where the trail left the beach, they began to climb the hills. This was hard, but Florence clung doggedly to the handles. She would not add her weight to the reindeer's load. During her weeks of training for this race, she had come to love these reindeer. They were small, but ever so plucky. Mile after mile they trotted on without a sign of weariness.

At the mouth of Tissue River, where they were again to go out upon the frozen beach, they learned to their dismay that they were being outpaced by Faye Mills and her team. "Have to step on it," the kindly old lodgekeeper encouraged.

Two miles from Tissue River Lodge, a strange thing happened. They were passing what appeared to be three snow-covered sand dunes when one of those dunes did an amazing thing. It stood up on four long legs, stuck out a very long neck, and stared at them.

Florence, who was riding at the moment, nearly fell from her sled. But, pointing a finger, Nowadluk called back laughingly:

"Big old white bear! Bet he never saw reindeer pull sled before."

"Isn't he dangerous?"

"If he is hungry, yes. Plenty seals now I think. Not hungry this one."

A minute had not passed before Florence knew that Nowadluk was wrong, for in long, easy lopes the bear began to follow them.

Gaining on us, too, the girl thought a moment later in sudden terror. *The deer are tired. They can't run fast.*

In this she was wrong, for—suddenly smelling the bear—the deer sprang over the trail at a speed Florence had never experienced before. The snow fairly flew. And yet as the girl watched, she realized that the bear still gained. It was both remarkable and terrifying, this strange new race in the arctic night.

Flashing her powerful electric torch upon the bear, the girl felt her heart give a sudden leap. He was immense, that bear—immense and gaunt, with deep sunken eyes. He seemed tireless. The deer were slowing down. How was it all to end?

Chapter three

As Florence sat on her sled, fascinated and frightened by the great white bear, strange tales told her by aged Eskimo hunters flashed through her mind. When seals were plentiful, the polar bear was peaceful, harmless. But when hunger stalked the land, so terrifying were the tales told about the great white bear that they brought chills of fright to her very bones.

Nowadluk was urging her deer forward. Florence's deer would follow the leader. There was no need for urging. The deer, thoroughly frightened by bear smell, were doing their best. Their speed had been redoubled.

Suddenly Florence let out a gasp, Nowadluk was slipping from her sled. She would run behind it, giving the deer more speed. As her feet touched the ground she began taking giant strides.

Could she, Florence, do that? She would try. But she must be careful! A slip of the hand, and all would be lost. Without that hold on the sled, she could not keep up with the deer. And then? She shuddered at the thought.

A careful glide, a sudden swing to the hard-packed snow, and—she had made it. Her feet came down in painful rhythm on the hard trail.

Strangely enough, at this moment a question flashed through her mind. *Why had the mysterious little man visited their village and their reindeer camp? Why had he been so very much interested in reindeer? Why had he not told them the purpose of his visit?*

But now a new sound broke in upon her senses. It was the sharp, angry bark of a dog.

"A dog!" she called aloud. "Way out here! No one within ten miles. He—"

She did not finish. Having turned half about, she swung her flashlight on the trail to see Faye Mills's golden collie dog, Stardust, defying the great white bear.

Swinging a foot or two to the right, ignoring the dog, the bear came straight on. The dog would have none of that. He was fast and canny. Ten seconds more and he was nipping at the giant's heels.

Without a sound the bear wheeled about, seized the dog with his ivory fangs, and sent him whirling far out over the ice.

"Oh!" the girl breathed. "That's the end of poor Stardust."

She was wrong. Apparently Stardust had but begun fighting. Having fallen like a rolling pin, he went tumbling over and over to at last scramble to his feet, shake himself, then renew the attack.

"Nowadluk!" Florence screamed. "Stop the deer! We can't let Stardust be killed!"

Nowadluk stopped the deer, then stared at her companion in bewilderment.

"Got no gun!" she exclaimed.

"Yes—yes! Something like a gun," was the white girl's astonishing reply.

Digging into her pack she dragged out a flash bulb camera mechanism her father had rigged up for her—the one that was to have taken pictures of the finish of the race.

"Perhaps the bear will think it's a gun," she murmured. "Anyway, it pops, and—"

She was away over the back trail.

"Not too far!" Nowadluk warned.

With a low howl of pain Stardust had just landed once again on the ice where he had been thrown. The bear, reared up on his hind legs, seemed immense. Coming not too close, Florence put a trembling finger to her flashlight button and pressed it hard.

For an instant there was no response. Would the thing fail her? Her heart sank. Then there came a low pop, and their whole world was aglow.

Quickly Florence replaced the burned-out bulb with another. The bear had dropped on all fours and was turning half about.

"Now!" she exclaimed. "When it pops you scream at the top of your voice!" Nowadluk understood. When again the world went all aglow, they both screamed. At that, the bear turned and went racing away to lose himself among the ice piles.

Stardust went limping gamely after him, but Florence called him back.

Just a minute later, with Stardust curled up beside her, the girl was once again speeding through the night.

A few moments of rest, then again she was trotting along behind her sled. As if understanding the importance of it all, Stardust, too, slipped from his place of comfort and went limping along beside her. When she would have put him back on the sled, he looked up at her as if to say, *Don't you think I can take it?*

"Good old Stardust!" she whispered, patting his head.

Silently, smoothly the miles slid by until as they rounded a long row of sand dunes they came to a welcome sight, an Eskimo's lighted tent glowing in the night.

"Whose tent is it?" Florence called to Nowadluk.

"Kitmesak. His tent."

"Tell him to take Stardust and keep him for us."

"All right. I tell him."

At Simrock they received the encouraging news that they were some minutes in the lead of Faye Mills, their nearest contender.

"You were behind," someone shouted. "Now you are ahead. How did you do it?"

"Assisted by a bear," Florence called back laughingly as they glided away into the night.

After that, they did not ride at all. Clinging to her sled, Florence trotted on and on. At times she was so nearly asleep that short, fantastic dreams flashed through her mind. At other times she was so painfully awake that the strain of the long run was torture.

At last, scarcely knowing what it meant, she began to see a light far ahead. This light grew until it filled all the sky. Then she knew it had to be a bonfire lighted by hundreds of interested spectators awaiting their arrival.

"Truly there is a great interest now in the reindeer of Alaska. Surely some good must come of it. Please, God," she prayed, "help us."

A rousing cheer greeted them as at last they passed the goal line.

* * * * *

The race was not won. It was but well begun. Faye Mills and her companion had an hour in which to catch up; the Bowman sisters had two hours.

When at last the time allotted for Faye to win had come and she had not yet crossed the goal line, Florence heaved a sigh almost of regret. There was little joy in winning against so wonderful a competitor. Faye finally came in, having lost by less than two minutes.

One more hour of waiting, and the race was won. The Bowman sisters lost by a full quarter of an hour.

"We must do this again," Winnie, the taller of the pair, exclaimed. "It's been loads of fun! And how it has wakened the old town up!"

"It has given Alaska grand publicity too," her sister added. "They say the papers are full of it."

"Oh! The pictures!" Florence exclaimed. "I meant to take some pictures, but we used up all my flash bulbs!"

"It won't matter," said Winnie. "Doffs, our photographer, took some as we came in—some of each team. But how did you use your flash bulbs?"

"You'd be surprised," Florence replied, allowing an air of mystery to creep into her voice. "But here's my camera. Perhaps Doffs will develop the film for me tonight. Then you can see."

"Oh. I'm sure he will. Let's hurry."

"May I have just a word?" a voice broke in on their conversation. It was the mysterious little man who had been rescued from the ice floe. "Allow me to congratulate you." He shook Florence's hand warmly.

"And now," he went on, "I have something to say to you and to that little girl who helped drive the Shishmaref team."

"Faye Mills," said Florence. "I'll call her."

"No! No! Not tonight!" the little man exclaimed. "This is not the setting. Everything must be done in the proper dramatic manner." He let out a low chuckle. "Suppose you and Miss Mills meet me at noon tomorrow in the lobby of the Golden Gate! Then we can have lunch together!"

"All—all right. That will be grand. I'm sure Faye will come." The girl's head was all awhirl. *Now I'm going to be told his secret,* she was thinking.

* * * * *

Florence was fairly bursting with curiosity as she and Faye met the stranger the next day. But the little man insisted on their full enjoyment of the meal before he said one word of real importance.

"And now!" he said, as all but the teacups had been cleared away. "Now to business. Until now I have said nothing of my mission in Alaska. I did not wish to set up false hopes."

"Hopes?" Florence whispered.

"You see," he went on, "I was sent here to study Alaskan reindeer, to discover the herd composed of the hardiest stock and the best-trained sled deer."

"But I don't see—"

The little man held up a hand. "You shall see, at once!" he laughed happily. "A few years ago," he went on, "the Canadian government imported some three thousand deer from Alaska. The experiment has been a success. Other natives, farther to the east, need reindeer as a food supply. I have been empowered to purchase these deer—two thousand in all."

"And—and you—" Florence could go no further.

"I have decided to select half our deer from the Shishmaref herd and half from the Wales herd."

"Oh! Oh!" the girls breathed in unison. In their minds figures were multiplying themselves. *One deer, fifteen dollars. One thousand deer—* What a boon to their people that would be! The old days of plenty would return. With proper care, this money might be made to last for years.

"I—I think it's wonderful!" was all Florence could say.

"Wonderful," Faye Mills echoed, turning her face away for a moment.

* * * * *

"A Race for an Unknown Prize," by Roy J. Snell. Published in The Girls' Companion, *Oct. 29, Nov. 5, and Nov. 12, 1939. Text printed by permission of Joe Wheeler (P.O. Box 1246, Conifer, CO 80433) and David C. Cook, Colorado Springs, CO 80918. Roy J. Snell, born in Laddonia, Missouri, in 1878, was a prolific author of books and stories for young people, titles such as* An Eskimo Robin Crusoe *(1917);* Told Beneath the Northern Lights *(1925); and* Wings for Victory *(1945).*

By
Dr. WILFRED T. GRENFELL.

BRIN

Wilfred T. Grenfell

Famed Canadian doctor Wilfred T. Grenfell remembers a most uncertain winter journey—uncertain because he didn't know the route. Only one sled dog had been on it before—and but once. Was Dr. Grenfell willing to risk their lives on mere possibility that the dog would remember?
Grenville wished he knew.

* * * * *

We were a hundred miles from a hospital, on the west coast of the long promontory of north Newfoundland that lies between two branches of the polar current. A fortnight since we had left our harbor of St. Anthony. As things had been quiet there, my new associate had decided to accompany me, in order that he might become familiar with the country which, next winter, he would have to travel alone. We were out giving our dogs an extra feed overnight, preparatory to starting back on the morrow.

It takes all the attention of two men to feed a team of husky dogs, if you wish to make sure that they share anywhere near alike. For not only is there a master dog, who takes all he wants anyhow, but each single dog knows exactly which of the others he can bully. It doesn't in the least matter how good a piece may fall to him, if he sees another with apparently a better, he will immediately fly at him.

The result often is that before they have settled the dispute, both pieces have vanished to their mates, and only fresh assaults and batteries will save the two contestants from going supperless.

Thus it happened our minds were so occupied that the approach of a large team of dogs from the north escaped our notice. Stimulated by the well-recognized signs of a meal, the new arrivals, turning deaf ears to the cries of the man who was driving them, and who was now clinging to the sledge with both hands for dear life, simply leaped into the middle of the fracas. Before a word could be said, the sledge was capsized, the driver was sprawling beneath it; and heaving, writhing, yelping masses of fur were enjoying the one attraction superior to a meal—a good, straight fight, quite regardless of the fact that the champions of one side were still tied to their sledge, and were rapidly snarling up themselves and everything else in an utterly inextricable tangle. It went greatly against the grain to have to whip our dogs off, but under the circumstances there was no alternative. Worse still, it left the victors in possession of the supper, when our sympathies were entirely with our own team.

This irritating incident had not materially helped us to appreciate the message that Joe, the driver of the new arrivals, blurted out as soon as the dogs were quieted.

"They is wanting you in Island Harbor, Doctor. They doesn't know what t' sickness be."

"Oh, that's it—eh? How long since you left?"

"Only two days, Doctor. I got as far as the Green Ridge tilt [or shelter hut] first night."

"Why, you came all around by the coast, didn't you?"

"Only as far as Caplin Cove Tickle. None of us had ever been straight across the Cloudy Hills. There be no track, and it's nigh impossible to find t' cut path through t' big woods from there out here unless you know every inch of it."

Now it couldn't be more than sixty or seventy miles across country to the place we wanted to reach, and it would be nearly twice that distance to go around. We could count on covering the former distance in a day, if only we could follow the trail. But that was just where the rub came. If you once lost it, it would be an endless task getting a team of dogs through the dense, stunted spruce forests with their windfalls of ages, which make them like one huge battle stockade, and with countless pitfalls, too, hidden under light snow coverings between the logs, where you only crawl over one to fall into the next. We had had more than one experience of that kind, and had had to abandon our sledges and exhausted dogs while, footsore and frozen, we struggled on without them.

It was a great dilemma. For not only did every sporting instinct cry out, "Have a fling at the cross-country route!" but success in the venture also meant that we should reach our desired haven a day sooner. *Could* we keep the trail?

Naturally, it was a topic of the evening as soon as our pipes were lit, and just as naturally half our friends were on one side and half on the other. But soon the crackling sound of footsteps on the crisp snow outside warned us of the approach of a newcomer.

The door was opened with the assurance of an old acquaintance, and a hearty chorus of welcome greeted the muffled figure that stopped to beat the snow off itself in the porch.

"Harry," said one, "you've just struck it right this time. Here's t' doctor wants to cross the country tomorrow. Can you help him?"

We found Harry had come in a hurry to get help to bring out two stags he had killed, and as he had not "scaffolded" them out of the reach of animals, he had to go right back in the morning.

"I'll tell you what I'll do, Doctor," he suddenly volunteered. "I won't see you left. If it *is* a bit of a round, I'll come with you as far as the big white marsh, and then if you'se don't get t'rough before dark, you'll surely find one of the Gray Cove men's tilts." And I saw his keen black eyes fixed on mine as if the sudden inspiration had relieved him of a burden.

"Thank you, Harry. That settles it, indeed, and try it we will, whatever comes of it."

It was unfortunate that my fellow doctor and I had decided to leave our usual driver at home on this trip, for he had crossed this very route the year previous. When we left, we had intended to return by the well-worn coast trail, in which case a driver's room would have been better than his weight on the sledges. We had left him, moreover, our good team of dogs, as there were a number of logs to be hauled home from the woods, more, indeed, than we could expect to handle before the going broke up. The result was, that of all our last year's team, we had only one dog with us, a yellowish brown dog with queer black-striped markings somewhat like a Bengal tiger. These lent to his sinister face the suggestion that he was eternally grinning—an impression intensified by an odd way he had of turning up the corners of his mouth when he caught one's eye. He went by the name of Brin.

I had reared this dog myself and run him his second winter as my leader, though he was then little better than a pup. On several occasions he had displayed unusual instinct for direction. Very soon after his first promotion, I had been compelled to run eighteen miles, mostly over sea ice, without seeing any intervening house, in a blizzard of snow and a head wind. It was quite impossible to do any steering, as the driving snow, with no windbreak, made seeing to windward out of the question. But the pup had proved his mettle by coming up without a hitch at the door of the house we wished to find, as it marked the spot where the shore trail turned to cross the neck of land. Thus, of all the party, Brin alone had ever seen the trail we were now proposing to take, and he had crossed it only once. It had, moreover, been very bad weather all the way. No one could say, of course, how much his memory could be counted on, but, personally, I was prepared to bank a good deal on it.

An hour or so more was spent in discussing the way. Indeed, I traced out a rough map of the trail according to Harry's ideas of it. Beginning with our present position, I drew in ponds, barrens, marshes, woods, as he called them out, and arranged them in order as he said the road led next to the right or left. It was a weird-looking picture when we finished it.

When it had received the final verdict, "It's as good as us can do," the company began to break up, and we lost no time in turning in, as we would have to be on foot before daylight if we hoped to "reach over" before dark.

The sky was overcast, and it was cold and still dark as we collected our dogs next morning for the long run across country. But they were well trained to respond to our call, and though hidden away in every conceivable corner, or under houses, or often buried in the snow, they were soon rubbing their noses against our hands.

Harry and his comrade, with a large team of their own that knew that section of the country like a book, made the running all morning, and as we were climbing most of the time, it was just as well for our teams that we had only one man on each sledge. Of course we had had to bring along our medical stores and good supplies.

Nothing of any particular interest transpired till we broke out from the woods by the Hanging Marsh about ten in the morning. Indeed, nothing well could, for the path was broken for us by our pilots. However, here they had to leave us, and we halted under some large spruce trees to boil a "mug of tea," while we received our final instructions. "It is all easy enough if you know it," were Harry's last words, as he bade us goodbye.

The main thing that interested me, however, while he was talking, was the fact that there wasn't a mark of any kind on the face of the Hanging Marsh. I had noticed that even the blazes on the trees near the houses, which were far more numerous and fresher than any we could hope to find for many miles to come, were so obscured by glitter, that is, ice frozen on the tree stems, that had we been without our pilots, we should have lost our way a dozen times already. As we chatted over a

cup of hot tea and a pork bun, that most delec-
table invention, as it won't freeze, however cold
the day may be, we dragged out the map which
we had made the night before.

Having pointed out that the direction in
which we must steer across the marsh was toward
a tall spruce that towered up in solitary state above the rest
of the trees, our good-natured guides returned on their tracks.
It was already obvious to both of us doctors that we had not
the slightest chance of finding the trail. Our only assets
were our pocket-compasses giving us the general direction, our axes to clear a path when we should
get stogged, a hopeful disposition which
never spoiled for troubles till they came
along, and—Brin.

Whether he knew his importance
or not at the moment, I never could
tell. But a light seemed to dance in
his eyes, and his queer face assumed
a fairly impish aspect as he strutted
about at the end of his long leading
trace. I remember he kept looking
back and grinning at us as he waited for
the word *go*.

"Don't say a word," shouted my chum from the sledge behind. "Let's see if
he'll head right—across the marsh anyhow."

"All right," I called back. "Mum's the word. GO!"

And we simultaneously cut the lines holding the sledges back to keep the excited dogs from running away before we were ready.

Prosaic as it may seem to others, it was a moment of real excitement to us when
Brin led off at a stretch gallop in an absolute line for the tall lone spruce. As we
whisked by it, I can almost swear he looked back at me and winked, and although
twelve fathoms away, I fancied I caught the sound of an unearthly chuckle from him.

The snow surface on these highlands was splendid, and the dogs were in a mood
to go. So we just "sat tight" and let them. For the trail now led through wooded
country, and we were Indians enough from years of experience to notice that we
were keeping to the old cut path, in spite of having to circumvent many snags in it.

Shortly, however, we struck more open country, and as the trees were now scattered like those in an orchard, the path might have been anywhere. We could only watch the dog, who, though he had slackened somewhat, was still trotting along merrily, and as unconcerned as if he hadn't yet discovered there was any problem to be solved. Somewhere about ten miles from the marsh, in just such a setting as we were now passing through, we had marked on our map that a forked juniper tree was standing by itself in the middle of a long lead. The top boughs had been stripped from it, and the skull and antlers of an old caribou fixed in the cleft.

The utter inaccuracy of the map had led me to forget this landmark, and I was more than surprised to hear my chum suddenly shout out, "There she is!"

"There's what?" I exclaimed.

"Why, the skull in the tree," he responded.

As we use no reins to guide the dogs, we rely entirely on our voices to swing them to the right or left. A good leader obeys instinctively even at top speed, without apparently taking notice otherwise. On this occasion we both thought Brin looked around and laughed. But even if he didn't, we did, for our spirits went up with a bound as we realized we were still all right, and another ten miles lay behind us.

A little later we passed the top ridge of the Cloudy Hills. Here the going was good, because there were no longer even scrub trees to worry us. Moreover, there could be no doubt of the right direction, as there was only one gap through which we could well go.

From the outlet of the gorge we should have seen the sea some twenty miles below us. But the shadows of evening were already drawn too close, and the sky was still overcast. There seemed to lie between us and our goal nothing but endless miles of rolling forest. It appeared folly to expect to get through before morning. Yet if we were going to camp at all, now was the time to get a shelter built while we could still see.

How much longer could we trust Brin? He had swung off almost at right angles after emerging from the pass and was now guiding his followers along the upper edge of the woods. It seemed at last as if he were seeking something and was uncertain where to enter. But he showed no doubt about what to do a minute later, for, without even slacking speed, he dashed into the forest. I looked back and caught the eye of my companion, and I saw he also had noticed a half-covered blaze on the trunk of a birch to the side of us. Down—down—down we went, the cut path every now and again obscured by growing saplings or blocked by windfalls which had to be carefully negotiated. But they counted for nothing beside the fact that every minute was shortening the distance, and we were obviously still on the track.

Time passes quickly steering a loaded sledge down through woods. You want all your skill and strength to steer clear of stumps and snags. Every now and again, even with the best of teams, some dog will turn the wrong side of an obstruction, and the whole team is suddenly brought up "standing." As a rule it is not a very long matter to haul back the prodigal, and sling him round after the others, though when he finds he is being dragged back, he just hauls for all he is worth, thinking he is going to be whipped. The presence of a new dog in the team, named Snowball, added a new and very definite element of trouble. For a sudden check would fling the dogs all together in a heap, and they seemed invariably to associate him with the cause of their last night's trouble, which they greatly resented. The unfortunate Snowball was, of course, forced to defend himself, and the process of separating the contestants often enough drove several more dogs around tree trunks. So that the fracas had to end by clearing them all out and making an entirely new start.

At the foot of the first range, the valley contained a long lake onto which we ran out squarely at right angles. Facing us was a steep bluff, and the lake seemed to end below in a narrow defile through which we guessed the river escaped, and toward which we, of course, expected to turn. But no such notion apparently entered Brin's head. He made exactly for the opposite direction, and then, crossing a narrow portion of the lake, started to climb the hill in front of us. The excellent engineering of this move became apparent only when, after a few moments, we were once more through a pass and discovered that we were at the head of a second valley that led in exactly the opposite way. No marks of any kind were visible, and it was now a long while since we had seen any indications that we were following a trail. We had hoped before this to see at least snowshoe marks of hunters from the coast. But nothing of that kind either was discernible. However, Brin continued to gallop down the sloping hillside, and there was nothing for us to do but "sit tight and look on."

As we swung around a big drift of snow, over an unusually large boulder, a very fresh fox track ran directly down "the bluff." Without once looking back, Brin jumped right into it, his unquestioning comrades following him only too gladly. The pace at once increased, and it seemed as if we were being made mere fools of, while the dogs had a good time hunting. It was mighty hard not to "butt in" and tell a "mere dog" which way to go. I looked round, however, to see whether my comrade had noticed the turn of events. "It's a case of walking by faith, I reckon," he shouted. "Do you suppose Brin knows what he's after?" The sound of his name evidently apprised the dog that we were discussing him, for even at the pace at which we were now going, he found time to fling his impish head around and fairly grin in our faces.

I never would have believed that an ordinary fox trail could cause so much worry for a man. But when we were still following that unspeakable beast's footsteps after a full mile had elapsed, it became almost impossible not to interfere. For the likelihood that a fox was really heading for the village we were seeking seemed absurd. All of a sudden this idea was apparently proven correct beyond the possibility of doubt, for we crossed the tracks of a man's snowshoes at right angles to our path. It was too much for us, so we halted the dogs, and, donning our own shoes, we followed the marks each way to see if they gave any clue as to how to proceed. Luckily for us, we soon found signs that the man was hunting, for his trail doubled on itself twice, and we knew he at least was not going in or out of the country.

"What's the best thing to do, John? There's still time to make a camp before dark. That fiend of a dog seems cock-sure of his way. But I don't know if the devil isn't in the beast. Look at his face. He looks possessed, if ever a dog did."

Brin was sitting bolt upright on his haunches and was staring directly at us— for all the world as if he understood exactly what we were saying. As he caught my eye, he put his head on one side and actually poked out his tongue. It was surely quite unnecessary to begin to pant just at that moment. But he maintained so inscrutable a mien, without even a blink, that though I half unconsciously picked up my whip as if to teach him to "quit fooling," I hadn't the heart to flick it.

It was getting late, and I felt we really ought to do something at once. "What do you say to blindfolding him? Perhaps then he'll leave this miserable fox track," I suggested.

"I'm for giving him another chance," was the trustful reply.

"All right, then. 'Barkis is willing,' " and I threw myself onto the sledge with a "Hist" to the dogs to go "just where they jolly well liked!" Bother, if they didn't again start off at a trot along that unspeakable fox track! But at last we came out onto the bed of the river, and I saw the fox tracks disappear into the willows.

It was with real relief that we proceeded to follow the river for a time. The low banks had allowed the wind to blow the snow away, and the resulting good ice surface, together with the drop of the stream, made it easy to cover the miles at our leisure. Moreover, we knew the river must lead to the sea sometime. Our hopes rose so high that we positively took the time to warm up the kettle and get our second "mug of tea" for the day. When we again started, the valley narrowed, and the riverbed was blocked with snow, while every here and there were great chasms that revealed the rushing water beneath. Worse still, the river ended abruptly in a huge lake with at least one large island in it. Nor was there the faintest indication now as to whether we should turn to the north, south, east, or west.

It seemed possible, however, to leave the east out of our reckoning, because in that direction we could see, across the lake, a high range of hills rising. Yet without hesitation Brin headed straight for them! On—on—on—till at last we came to the woods flanking the lake. The dogs instantly went straight into the forest, and in half a minute were on opposite sides of a dozen trees.

"That settles it, John. The sooner we make a shelter for the night the better," I said, as I started to find a dry tree with which to light a fire.

John stood ruefully looking at the dogs. Apparently, he had counted even more on Brin than I had, and he said afterward he felt as if the bottom had fallen out of his faith in everything. The dogs, glad of a rest, lay down where they were and started chewing the icicles out of their fur. Brin alone, who was at the end of the longest trace, had it stretched out to its full length, and so he was nearly hidden by the bushes. But I could see he was standing up and looking back as he used to when the team slacked and he was accustomed to come back and snap at them. His odd manner influenced me enough to start off in his direction after I had turned over the ledge. To my amazement, I found he was standing in a well-cut path which ran at an acute angle up to the side of the hill! He had tried a shortcut into it, about ten yards before it opened onto the lake!

There was no trouble after this. Once over the hill, we struck the wood path of the Gray Cove men, and by 8:00 p.m. had brought up outside my patient's house. We were both able to tell "what t' sickness was" and to be of some service.

Before turning in, I went out to see what the night was like and to make sure that Snowball was safely fastened up. For I knew he would steal home again the moment he got the chance. Everything was all right, however, and the tired dogs were stowed away somewhere asleep. My hand was on the latch of the cottage door, and I was about to reenter and turn in, when something warm and furry rubbed gently against my leg. By the light that streamed out of the open door, I found myself looking right down into Brin's eyes. They were asking, in as plain English as could be written, "How did I please you today, Master?" I couldn't help putting my arms around his neck and hugging him! Then we both went off to our beds the happier for it.

* * * * *

"Brin," by Wilfred T. Grenfell. Published in St. Nicholas, *Dec. 1911. Original text owned by Joe Wheeler. Sir Wilfred Grenfell, MD (1865–1940), pioneer medical missionary to Labrador, was one of the most celebrated humanitarians of his time. Among his books are* Vikings of Today *(1895),* A Labrador Doctor *(1919), and* The Romance of Labrador *(1934).*

THE PILGRIMS OF THE SKY

Samuel Scoville Jr.

The golden eagle, king of the sky, is so powerful he can kill—in midair—any bird that flies.

So what chance did the great whistling swan have, steadily migrating north at a mile a minute? Was he unaware of his impending doom?

* * * * *

Honk! Honk! Honk! The sound drifted down from a wedge of wild geese beating their way northward up the sky, and shouting to earth as they flew.

The beech trees were all lavender-brown and silver, the fields of wheat made patches of brilliant, velvety green against the Connecticut hills, the woods dripped green, and the new leaves of the apple trees were like tiny jets of green fire among the pink-and-white blossoms. And the Pilgrims of the South were on their way home.

As the flock crossed Coltsfoot Mountain, they came close to earth over Coltsfoot Farm, that long green valley which the Calhouns of Connecticut had owned for generations. From the farmyard, a flock of tame geese stretched forth their long necks, raised their wings, and honked back at their wild brethren bound for their nesting grounds in the North, where the marshes were still gray with ice.

Among the earth-bound flock was a young gander who had been shot down

CHARLES LIVINGSTON BULL

with a broken wing the year before. John Calhoun's farmer had clipped his long wing feathers and put him in with the tame geese. Unnoticed, the primary feathers on his wings had grown again after his last moulting. Today, when he heard the call of his brethren, he called back to them and flapped his wings. Suddenly he felt that his power was upon him once more. With a sweep of his mighty vans, he launched himself forth into the air in a long curve, shot up through the sky, and in a moment had taken his place in the right-hand side of the V, just back of the old gander who led the flock—and his earth-bound companions saw him no more.

Far above the geese, in the upper reaches of the sky, above the storms and the clouds themselves, in naked space, a company of whistling swans was traveling. All that day and the next night they hurtled toward the North at the rate of nearly a mile a minute, untiring, unresting. Other travelers, who were following the paths of the air below them, heard through the dark, at intervals, calls like the notes of a clarinet far, far above them, and were heartened in their flight, knowing that the kings of the sky were on their way to the tundras, which stretch beyond the farthest forests of the North to the Arctic Circle itself.

* * * * *

Next morning the rays of the rising sun fell upon the flock just as they were crossing the Canadian border and turned the flying swans into birds of silver. Snow-white, with black bills and feet, they were nearly two feet longer than the geese, with a far wider wing-expanse. Then, as the sun rose higher and higher, the flock of swans suddenly seemed to lift in their flight, and in a long upward slant, moved toward the blue vault which hung over them in the morning sunlight like a dome of incandescent turquoise. No human eye could have distinguished those misty white shapes gliding across the highest range of the Laurentian Mountains. Yet from the summit of a peak two eyes—not human—did see them, eyes like molten gold, with a telescopic vision, in whose fixed gaze was the fierce arrogance which only that imperial *Raptore,* the golden eagle, possesses.

For an instant the great bird watched the swans with veiled, inscrutable vision, motionless as if carved from the rock on which he perched. Then, without a preliminary motion or flutter of his wings, he launched himself into space, and spiraled up through the clouds.

In a minute he had reached a level above that held by the shining wedge of swans and settled down to overhaul the gleaming pilgrims from the South.

Although an eagle has not the swiftness of the duck hawk of America, or the peregrine falcon of Europe, yet there are few birds who can outfly him when he strikes his hunting gait.

Perhaps it was the hiss of driven air through the vast pinions of the eagle that the old leader of the swans heard, above the harplike tones of the wings of his flock. Perhaps he turned his wary head—but whether warned by sight or sound, this much is certain: he was aware of the coming of the eagle long before that sky king had reached the flock. Yet the great swan imperturbably maintained, unchanged, the journey pace which he had set throughout the long pilgrimage from the South, nor increased by a single beat the steady strokes of his singing wings.

There are two ways by which the hunters of the air secure their prey. One is that used by the falcons, who fly above the hunted bird and, dropping down upon it like a meteor, dash the life from the fugitive by one tremendous blow of the knuckles of their closed talons. The other method is that of the goshawk, who "binds" his prey. From above he drives his curved talons deep into the flesh of his victim and then goes to earth with it, the keen claws piercing to the very life of the bird which he has seized. An eagle employs the same system, and his fatal talons are long enough to kill, in midair, any bird that flies, while the driving power of his huge pinions is such that he can carry even a swan to his aery without descending to earth with it.

There was something about the grim unconcern of the silvered birds which would have given pause to any other of the *Raptores*. The golden eagle, however, by his very nature, never admits that any bird is his equal, and moreover this Laurentian king of the air had never chanced to encounter swans before. In an instant he had traversed the whole length of the V in which the swans were traveling and hung poised above the grim and wary leader, the largest and most powerful of all of his company. The silver bird neither quickened nor slackened his pace, but regarded his opponent inscrutably out of his gleaming black eyes, while with no sign of confusion or alarm, the rest of the flock dropped back.

In the full light of the sun, a mile above the earth, beneath the unclouded blue dome of the sky, the plumage of the eagle gleamed as if inlaid with burnished gold, and rivaled in brightness the silver-white of the swan below. Suddenly, without a movement of his great wings to announce the attack, the sky king shot down toward the swan like some gleaming projectile, his hooked beak half-open, his deadly talons outspread and ready to pierce deep into the body of the bird below.

Neither the blunt bill of the swan nor his webbed feet were available for defense, but he possessed one weapon quite as effective as the eagle's claws. Even as the great *Raptore* struck, the swan whirled in midair, evading the fatal clutch of his opponent, and at the same instant delivered a tremendous blow with one of his gleaming wings, which caught the plunging bird like the full-armed swing of a boxer. The wing stroke of a swan has been known to break a man's leg and to kill a wolf outright, and this one in a second transformed the fierce, swift figure of the eagle into a crumpled mass of gold-and-brown feathers. One wing feebly flapped and the other was disabled and dangling as the bird fell slowly down toward the peak whence he had come. The speeding flock above stared down at him impassively and continued their uninterrupted journey.

* * * * *

Beyond the meeting place of the eagle and the swans the mountain range towered to the clouds. There, amid a waste of rocks and ice, through that gateway of the North, came a swift bird with a black head, pearl-gray wings, and a forked white tail, who had flown from the desolate Antarctic ocean—the Arctic tern, who holds the long-distance record of the world.

Perhaps, during those ten thousand miles from the wastes that ring the South Pole around, the wanderer had lost his mate. Perhaps he was a solitary pioneer of the brave band who, following a route unknown to man, travel from pole to pole, and have nearly eight months of daylight out of every year. Whatever the reason, he flashed through the sky alone. High above the highest peaks, disdaining storms and mists and clouds alike, he relied upon that undiscovered compass which guides all bird folk, even when blinded, across uncharted seas and unknown lands; while a marvelous engine, far more powerful than any of human contriving, drove his light, swift body across the world, for long days at a time, on a few ounces of fuel.

The swans, the geese, and the various tribes of the ducks travel fast, as do the golden plover, who take the water route up from the Argentine, across the treacherous Gulf and the storm-swept Atlantic, twenty-four hundred miles to the shores of Nova Scotia, their first stop. The Arctic tern, however, travels at a swifter pace than any of them. It seemed incredible that such a bird, moving like a flash of silver above the earth, need fear any winged thing. Yet as he crossed the highest peak of the range, down from a fleecy cloud drifted what seemed at first to be a wisp of floating mist. Only when it had detached itself from the cloud where it had been lurking did it appear as a white bird, faintly dappled with fine bars of semilunes of gray. Its fierce, glittering black eyes and hooked, black-tipped beak marked it as the white gerfalcon, the fastest bird of prey that flies. He had drifted down from far beyond the Arctic Circle and was haunting that mountain gateway of the North, lurking amid the high clouds, to steal forth and prey upon northbound travelers as they passed beneath him.

With an effortless motion the falcon shot from his hiding place, swift as a shooting star. He seemed to move his long vans languidly—yet he was doing three feet to the tern's two, and the chase had only begun.

Some saving instinct caused the tern to look up. One glimpse, and the wanderer knew that death itself was approaching. Although he had traveled thousands of miles without rest or food, he shot forward through the lower reaches of the sky with a burst of incredible speed. As he flew, he circled and doubled in dizzying, puzzling loops. But always the falcon followed closely his every twist and double and circle, with a speed which brought him nearer and nearer.

Unable to evade his grim pursuer by such tactics, with a loud *tu-err, tu-err, tu-err* the tern flashed straight away across the mountain range, but with long, easy sweeps of his curved and pointed wings the gerfalcon followed.

Little by little the tern's long days of speeding through the air without food or rest began to tell. His pace slowed until at last the great hawk hung directly over him. Before the fierce bird could strike, however, the tern veered in midair and flew desperately downward toward the peaks and valleys of the mountain range, as if it preferred the rocks below to the cruel talons of the gerfalcon. In a long flash of white and gray the two whizzed down from the high sky like twin meteors.

The fugitive passed the pinnacle of the range. Through the deep valley suddenly blew a blinding snowstorm, and in a second the fleeing bird was in the center of its smother and whirl. In the impenetrable whiteness of fast-falling flakes, the tern circled down the deep gorge and found safety. On a little ledge, beneath an overhanging cliff, it waited out the storm. Later on, under cover of the darkness, star-guarded, the pilgrim of the South once again resumed his interrupted journey to the Far North where, a few degrees from the very pole itself, he would meet a glorious mate and raise a brood in solitude, where man nor beast has ever penetrated.

Soon after the escape of the tern, after many advances and retreats, spring came north to stay, and the sky, from the Gulf to the Canadian border, was filled night and day with vast caravans of birds returning home.

* * * * *

On a day early in spring came the swifts, who take their name from their flight—coming from an unknown country, for no man has ever discovered where they go when they cross the Gulf on their journey south.

Stripped for speed, fearing no foe, they whirled across the Gulf in a great cloud with black streamers on either side and followed the eastern coast north, feeding as they went on whatever insects they encountered in the air. Some time during that month they would reach their homes, scattered through the Eastern States all the way to the Canadian border. Then, breaking tiny, dead twigs in mid-flight from the tops of trees, they would gum them together into little crescent-shaped nests, fastened to the inner walls of unused chimneys by a sticky secretion exuded from their bills, and raise their two nestlings there in the dark.

* * * * *

With the swifts came the swallows, day fliers also. Blue, white-bellied tree swallows, with brown bank swallows and rough-winged swallows; cliff swallows with cream-white foreheads, and the barn swallows with long forked tails—the air was full of their curving flight. As they flew it did not seem as if any winged creature could equal their speed. Yet as they crossed the Gulf and sped northward, a shadowy flier, wearing soft fur that gleamed like silver in the sun, followed the speeding flock. On bare wings covered with a tough, leathery membrane, and with a spread of over two feet, a hoary bat, the largest of his kind, was migrating with the swallows. Soon, however, in spite of their flashing speed, he overtook the flock and passed them all, for skin makes a better flying surface than feathers.

The swallows and swifts had no more than passed by when the sky was full of the clamor and clangor of ducks. The canvasbacks, with dark-red heads and necks, grunted as they flew. The goldeneyes whistled; the black ducks and the mallard drakes, with emerald-green heads, quacked; the pintails whimpered; the tiny blue-winged teal gave a soft lisping call, and the swifter green-winged teal sounded their mellow flute notes.

On and on—until they had flown the sun out of the sky and darkening shadows on the earth below showed like spilt ink in the violet twilight. All through that night they headed for the polestar, above leagues and leagues of pine lands and many a marsh and morass—north and north. At last a turquoise day dawned, and winding streams on the earth below gleamed in sheets of sapphire and pools of molten silver, as the sun rose over miles of rushes, which hissed and rustled in the wind. There, among the pools of gray-green water, were the nesting-places that had called the duck folk from a thousand miles away.

* * * * *

During the last Ice Age, the ancestors of all of these fliers learned to migrate, going south as the ice increased and returning north when it melted. Although ice and glaciers and frozen heights have been gone thousands of years and more, the migration habit still persists.

Today there are several definite routes that are patronized by different birds. There is the twenty-four-hundred-mile water route from the Argentine, which only the aces of the air can follow. Some of the fainter-hearted fliers choose the island route, which leads across the Antilles, Puerto Rico, and Cuba, and so across the Gulf. It is an easy route, for those who follow it need never be out of sight of land, but it is long, and the table is not good. Another way is the Jamaica route, which stretches from South America to Florida, via Jamaica and Cuba. Some sixty different species of birds follow it.

The most traveled, because it is the most direct, is the Gulf route, directly across the Gulf of Mexico to northwestern Florida, a flight of seven hundred miles without a stop. Millions of birds take it. Even the rails—whose wings are so small that for a long time it was thought that they migrated on foot—in spite of their bumbling, uncertain flight prove themselves on the Gulf route. So do the ruby-throated hummingbirds, the smallest of all North American birds, who fly so swiftly and are so tiny that they show only as specks in the air. Yet they cross the Gulf unafraid, although it would seem as if a breath of mist would clog those tiny, whirring wings.

This year the first flights of all of the pilgrims had gone north before the eagle had been worsted by the swan. The great horned owl, who nests in February, and the northern raven were rearing their hardy broods amid snow and ice. That dauntless trio—first migrants to appear in our Eastern States—the purple grackle, the robin, and the bluebird, had been joined by the phoebe, the kingfisher, the red-winged blackbird, the vesper and field sparrows, and a score of other early comers.

Then came a night when a great wave of the travelers from the South passed through.

The upper air was full of tiny pipings and chirpings. Across the face of the moon showed a multitude of black, moving dots. The night fliers were calling back and forth, heartening each other as they flew through the long, dark hours. These were the stout-hearted birds who were taking the bobolink route from South America, six hundred miles across the Caribbean Sea to Cuba, and then on to Florida and up the Atlantic Coast.

There were hosts and myriads of bobolinks; cuckoos bound for New England; gray-cheeked thrushes for Canada; bank swallows for Labrador; blackpolls on their way to the Magdalen Islands; black-throated blue, golden-winged, yellow, and black-throated green warblers, all traveling together in the dark. With them went the veeries, the fly-catchers, the sparrows, the rails, the tanagers, and many other species, in separate companies. Their vast caravan filled the sky. In the darkness the travelers need not fear the attacks of those pirates of the air, the hawk folk, and that night there were no fogs to confuse them or storms to drive them out to sea, as often happens at this season.

Suddenly, as they followed the coastline, a great bar of white light swept like a flaming sword across their path. A lighthouse had been set in stormy seas, to guard the lives of human sailors. Tonight, as the vanguard of the bird host reached the light, some of them, bewildered by its glare, dashed themselves to death against the tower. Others flew around and around, like moths about a flame, and eventually would have dropped from exhaustion into the waves below. Fortunately for them all, however, at midnight the light changed to a beam of blood-red. Instantly the spell was loosed, and the pilgrims pursued their course away from the enchanted ground, freed from the spell of the white witch-fire.

All that night they flew, calling to each other through the darkness, never resting, never stopping. At dawn, from high overhead, came down to them a triumphant trumpet call. Through a glory of crimson and flame, six gleaming, misty-white birds of unearthly beauty flew across the eastern sky in strong, majestic flight. They were glorious trumpeter swans, largest of their race.

As these dwellers in the loneliest places of earth passed overhead, far, far below them the soft air was full of robin notes, bluebird calls, and the shrill, high notes of the hylas, like jangled silver bells.

The valleys were a blaze of green, and the woods were spangled with blue porcelain petals of the hepatica. There were clumps of snowy bloodroot, whose frail blossoms the wind kisses and kills; patches of fragrant trailing arbutus; great drifts of innocents. As the little pilgrims settled down to rest, Spring herself was waiting to welcome them.

* * * * *

"The Pilgrims of the Sky," by Samuel Scoville Jr. Published in St. Nicholas, *June 1931. Original text owned by Joe Wheeler. Samuel Scoville Jr. wrote nature stories for popular magazines during the first half of the twentieth century.*

LITTLE BAPTISTE

Raymond Thompson

Big Baptiste was a legend in the North Country, but now he was no more. It was just too bad that Little Baptiste failed to measure up to his illustrious sire. But desperate situations demand desperate measures.

* * * * *

Anne Beaudre stepped to the door of her father's trading-post store and looked anxiously across the swift mountain stream, hoping against hope to see the men returning from the Athabasca flats where the forest fire had been raging. The acrid smell of smoke was heavy in the Baptiste River Valley.

A small yellow husky sprang upon her, whining eagerly. "Down, Little Baptiste! I can't let you loose, old fellow! You couldn't do the fire fighters any good even if you did swim the river!" She pushed the dog away, suddenly noticing that for once the animal was not interested in the south trail across the river. Little Baptiste was looking toward the north.

Presently, through the haze, a slender native lad appeared, running with the easy swing of a "moccasin telegraph" messenger.

"Louie! What is it?" demanded the white girl, a new fear clutching at her heart.

"Little Smoky place—she burn down! Fire spread all over valley. Must get word to Mounted Police!"

"The Seevers!" Anne gasped, thinking of the family of her friend, Emily. Mr. Seever owned the trading post at the Little Smoky River crossing.

"The Seevers have escape, but their place ees all destroy!" Louie declared dramatically. "But unless the fire ranger come with help, all the beeg timber along the rivaire ees gone!"

Word must be sent out to the Mounted Police so that men could come in from the Big Smoky country and fight the new fires! The work her father and brother and the settlers along the Athabasca River were doing was of no avail against this sudden attack from an entirely different angle.

"Your brother Rolf. Maybe he can get word to the Mounties," Louie suggested eagerly.

Anne paused before reentering the store. "Please, Louie, don't say anything in front of Mother. She isn't at all well."

The Cree lad was already aware that something was wrong. He turned as Little Baptiste sniffed at his ankles. "Rolf—he ees gone! You tie up the Leetle Baptiste so he not follow?"

"Yes," Anne replied, hastily explaining how her father and brother had crossed the river by flatboat several days ago. The boat was now on the other shore. "I doubt if the dog would try swimming the river now, Louie. It's crept up four or five feet since Rolf and Dad left. There's no way we could cross the stream without a flatboat. But"—suddenly hopeful—"couldn't you go north to the mission and get help?"

"Non!" declared Louie in hushed tones, as they suddenly heard Anne's mother coming through the store. "The fire is much too bad. The Mounties must get word by what you call the telegraph to their northern posts. Then they come down the river by the beeg raft to fight the fire. We cannot raft upstream against the current. Do you see, my friend?"

"I see," Anne whispered, answering her mother's call with a cheery, "Coming! Louie is here to say that the Seevers are all right!"

* * * * *

The smoke seemed to hang more heavily than ever. At times it became so dense as to make breathing difficult even with dampened rags held to the face.

Louie was sitting on the river bank holding Little Baptiste's chain. Watching them, Anne thought of a possible solution to their difficulty.

"Little Baptiste!" she called sharply—then directly to Louie, "do you think he could make it?" pointing to the river.

The young Cree shrugged his shoulders. "Leetle Baptiste ees not beeg lak hees father before heem! I am afraid he would drown in the rapids just below!"

* * * * *

Anne felt sorry for Little Baptiste. Her brother Rolf was always comparing him with Big Baptiste, the father of the smaller husky. Rolf had been very proud of the huge dog. Far and wide in the Athabasca country had spread the fame of Big Baptiste—the sled and trail dog without an equal. And then one day from the track of a grizzly bear the animal had never returned. But he had left a six-month-old son—like him in everything but size. Rolf could scarcely wait for the pup to grow.

But Little Baptiste had already attained his full height! True, he broadened at the shoulders and was amazingly strong for his stature. But, lacking weight, he could not command the respect from other dogs and thus failed to assume the leadership formerly taken by Big Baptiste. *Rolf was a little indifferent to the son,* Anne thought.

"You know, Louie," she mused, "if I were Little Baptiste, I'd give a great deal for a chance to prove myself. He's been whining for three days because Rolf wouldn't take him along!"

"You mean?" inquired the native.

"I mean to give him his chance. Quick, Louie, a very light pack; and be sure that it doesn't bind his muscles. I will write a letter to Rolf and enclose it in a small bottle!"

"But the rapids?"

"We will take him downstream below them. The river is wider there but fairly smooth. I think he can swim it!"

Little Baptiste was so excited when they placed the pack on his quivering shoulders, Anne had to laugh outright.

By cutting across a bend in the river flats, it was a short half mile to the end of the rapids that commenced immediately below their boat landing.

"Maybe he has change hees mind!" Louie declared as they stood beside the wide swollen stream.

Little Baptiste was acting queerly. The pack adjusted, Anne had released him with a word of encouragement. He made a few short leaps and stopped at the water's edge, whining uneasily. Then he looked up and down the river bank.

"Now what?" Anne moaned. "You're right, Louie. He's looking for a boat. But we can't blame him if he doesn't understand."

The girl was holding out an old jacket belonging to her brother. The dog acted as though he understood what was required of him. In fact, several times he made for the river as if about to plunge in. Anne couldn't believe he was afraid.

Finally she sighed. "Poor fellow, we've kept him chained for so long he doesn't know just what to think. Well, there's no reason to keep him chained now, Louie. Take off his pack!" She started dejectedly toward the post.

Suddenly she heard a shout behind her. "Mees Anne! Look! The Leetle Baptiste!"

She whirled. Little Baptiste was in the river, swimming strongly, headed for the opposite shore. His head was bobbling like a cork in the swift stream!

Louie was looking ruefully at the small pack in his hands—the pack that contained the precious message to Rolf Beaudre. "I just take off hees pack and turn my head. Then—splash—I hear heem hit the water."

Anne dug a pair of binoculars from the depths of her rucksack. Quickly she trained them on the river.

"The water is much rougher than we thought!" she breathed. "Do—do you think he can make it?"

She strained her eyes to follow Little Baptiste's course downstream. A sharp cry of relief escaped her parted lips. Far down, just above the break where another series of treacherous rapids commenced, she saw the brave animal crawl wearily ashore, staggering weakly.

"He made it, Louie! I'm glad he's safely across—even if he does us no good now. There! He's shaking himself and heading for the woods!"

"You think Rolf not know why we send heem Little Baptiste?"

Anne had turned toward home. "He won't even know that we did send him. Rolf will probably figure we turned him loose and that he took to the river of his own accord. But don't blame yourself, Louie. I told you to take the pack off. There's nothing we can do but wait for the men to come home. You can fix up a bunk in the fur cache!"

* * * * *

About noon several days later a Cree came down the trail from the north. He talked volubly with Louie, and the latter interpreted his message to Anne and her mother.

The Mounted Police had organized a large fire fighting force in the north and had come down in time to rescue the Seevers from almost certain starvation, since they had been cut off from a food supply. The men had also gained control of the worst fires. Louie didn't know how the Mounted Police had happened to come.

At sundown the same evening they heard a furious barking out on the river. "Dad and Rolf!" screamed Anne. "They have two dogs with them in the flatboat, and one is Little Baptiste!"

Anne and Louie were waiting for the boat to land. And Anne, after the first joyous greetings, noticed that the second dog was bandaged over one eye. He was a huge beast, and he limped as he walked. Little Baptiste leaped about as lively as ever.

"It ees heem!" Louie exploded, pointing to the animal whose feet had been burned and whose one eye blinked curiously.

"Right, Louie," Rolf declared solemnly. "It is Big Baptiste! He just turned up one day while we were fire fighting. He has been crippled and is mighty thin!"

Anne explained how they had tried to send a message by Little Baptiste. "But of course it didn't do any good," she finished, patting Little Baptiste.

"Oh, but you're wrong there, Sis," Rolf interposed hastily. "When Little Baptiste reached us, I felt uneasy. I climbed to the divide between the two rivers that one day the air was clear. I could see that everything was all right at the post. But to the north there were three distinctly bad fires, and I was sure that Seevers were cut off from coming to our post. So we spread the alarm by telegraph to the Mounted Police. Little Baptiste will be a real hero in this country!"

"Even if he wouldn't 'savvy' when we first tried to get him to carry a message in his pack. He just sat down at the water's edge and howled. Louie had taken off his pack and was starting for home when Little Baptiste suddenly changed his mind and plunged into the river!"

Rolf laughed heartily. "That's one on you, Sis. You've accused me of neglecting Little Baptiste, and right here's some proof of the training I gave him!"

"What do you mean?"

"Simply that a well-trained pack dog will never get into water with his load. He waits for his master to relieve him of it. That's why he plunged into the river the instant Louie took off his pack!"

Anne's eyes were bright. "And what about Big Baptiste?"

"He was terribly mauled by that grizzly and got his feet badly burned too. We'll pension him off to easy jobs. Little Baptiste can uphold the family traditions from now on," Rolf declared proudly.

* * * * *

"Little Baptiste," by Raymond Thompson. Published in Girls' Companion, *August 13, 1939. Text printed by permission of Joe Wheeler (P.O. Box 1246, Conifer, CO 80433) and David C. Cook, Colorado Springs, CO 80918. Raymond Thompson wrote for popular magazines during the first half of the twentieth century.*

The Feud on Swiftwater

William Gerard Chapman

Gabe Shaddick had every reason to hope for a good trapping season. Only problem was there was a wolverine on the prowl that was smarter than he was.
So the stalemate continued.

* * * * *

A low-hung, coppery sun glimmered dully through the uprearing, naked boles of pine and spruce and hemlock, laying long, purplish shadows across the white-carpeted floor of the winter wood as the twilight deepened. The wild feathered life of the forest fluttered into nest or cranny or thicket, seeking safe haven from the night prowlers that would soon be abroad. Their sleepy twitterings, blending with the soft whisper of the trees, made a drowsy monotone that hung pleasantly on the cold, crisp air, until of a sudden it was hushed in a wave of silence as two terrifying forms came hurrying down twin aisles of the forest.

Nearly abreast, and loping along at a swift pace, their approach sent the tardiest dwellers of the wood palpitatingly to cover. The larger figure, in rough homespun, rabbit-skin cap, and high moccasins thrust into the thonged hold of snowshoes, swept on as silently as the smaller, save for the crunch of his webbed footgear on the dry snow. The other, slightly to the rear of the man and hidden from his eyes by an artfully selected, twisting path that took advantage of every

tree trunk and bush and shadow, was a squat, surly-visaged animal, reminiscent of both bear and marten. Its small, dim-sighted eyes, glowering evilly from low brows fringed thickly with hair, seldom left the man as the wolverine kept pace with him by a series of seemingly awkward movements, its back arching with the curious undulations of a measuring worm as it jumped and shambled silently through the wooded maze.

The man was returning to his cabin after an inspection of one of his traplines, anger and humiliation written flamingly upon his face as a result of what he had discovered, and a seething thirst for vengeance in his heart. Constantly he swept his glance to right and left as he strode along. At times he stopped suddenly and turned, freezing into immobility while he peered back along his trail. But he could discern nothing of the black, ominous shape that on each occasion shrouded itself instantly within the impenetrable gloom of tree or bush and froze into an equal movelessness. The man felt, with the sixth sense of the woodsman, that he was being followed. A faint, but lively, shiver traveled up and down his spine and prickled at the roots of his hair—not a sensation of fear, but an uncanny premonition that malignant eyes were following his every move.

Without having heard the slightest sound of his companion of the trail, or so much as glimpsed its sinister shadow, he emerged from the timber at the tiny clearing in the fork of two ice-bound streams, and viewed the homely portal of his hut with a grunt of relief. Ordinarily he would have given but little thought to the affair, but today he was in a mood to be annoyed, for his mind was in a perturbed state over recent happenings on his traplines.

The wolverine halted at the edge of the clearing, flattening itself into perfect concealment at the roots of a low-spread balsam fir. As the trapper approached the cabin, he turned and shook his fist toward the black wall of trees in a mixture of anger and grim homage as he anathematized the clever miscreant who had played such havoc with his traps, and who was, he shrewdly surmised, eyeing him arrogantly from the dense growth. He was right in his conjecture, for the animal that had dogged his steps for miles and whose wicked little black eyes were appraising him maliciously from its hidden vantage was the same evil-dispositioned "Injun devil" that had made a mockery of his fur-taking endeavors for several days past.

At his door the trapper scanned again the black edge of the trees, and the lines of his face curved into an expression of guile. "Jest you git busy to-morrer with the traps, old feller, me boy. Mebbe ye'll find a surprise awaitin' ye!" With which cryptic remark he entered the cabin.

When Gabe Shaddick had come to the forks of the Swiftwater two weeks before, for a season of trapping, the wolverine instantly became aware of his arrival and set itself to the task, highly agreeable to its demon nature, of studying the man and his methods, to the end that life should be made miserable for this trespasser upon its domain.

On several occasions Gabe had felt the weird sensation of being followed and stared at by unfriendly eyes. Then one day he awoke swiftly to the menace that threatened his undertaking. Hardly a trap on the line that paralleled the east branch of the stream had been overlooked by a devastating agency whose tracks, for the first time, insolently mingled with his own and spelled plainly to the trapper the name of his opponent.

A marten "set" had been neatly uncovered, the trap sprung, and the bait stolen. Of his next set there was nothing to be seen. A disturbance of the snow and a few tufts of dark fur were sufficient evidence of what had occurred. The trap was nowhere in sight.

"Couldn't even leave me the trap, drat him! That was a prime marten-fur he et up an' done me out of," he muttered.

Wise in the ways of the black thief, he followed a broad trail which penetrated the brush at right angles to the line. At the distance of several rods it entered the growth of a low, thick-foliaged spruce; and casting his gaze searchingly into the mass of green, Gabe was rewarded by a sight of the clog—a heavy billet of wood to which the end of the chain was fastened. Kicking off his snowshoes, he wallowed on hands and knees to the base of the bushy tree, pulled his trap from the mound of snow under which it was buried, and backed out, with remarks appropriate to the occasion. Resetting the trap at another spot, he continued his course along the line.

His mind was now prepared for any shock of discovery. He knew how thorough an "Injun devil" could be in its career of mischief, and he was in nowise disappointed in its expectations. For each snare and deadfall, as well as trap, had been visited by the marauder, examined with crafty eye and paw, and robbed or demolished or stolen with a most uncanny proficiency. Gabe reset such of them as were not past further usefulness, recovering one more trap from its cache, this time a hollow log, and finally arrived at the end of the line, where he halted to give full expression to his thoughts. After his first outburst he had not had time—or breath—to do justice to his outraged feelings, for his hurry to learn the worst and the repeated evidence of the wolverine's devilment had held him in a grim and silent fascination.

"I'll git ye yet!" he growled, shaking a threatening fist aloft; and then his anger subsided as a grin persisted in breaking through the frown that seamed his face. "Ye're a right smart varmint, sure 'nough," he conceded with reluctant admiration; "hain't no other critter can hold a candle to ye fer downright cussedness, but ye've got a brain that some humans might better swop their own fer.

"Ye hain't agoin' to drive me off'n my trappin' grounds though," he asserted. "Me an' you'll fight this here thing out, an' see who's boss o' the woods."

Gabe started on the trail back to camp, muttering his vexation as he went. He planned many schemes for reprisal, and during the succeeding days put them to the test; but to no avail. His wily antagonist evidenced an ability to penetrate the secret of each well-planned trick to catch him unawares with a wisdom that seemed almost supernatural to the dismayed trapper. But the dogged nature of the backwoodsman held him to his determination to fight the affair to an issue, and the feud between man and beast continued unabated in energy and wit for the space of many weeks. However well planned his endeavors, Gabe failed to surprise his rival at his knavery.

When, on the night of his veiled threat, the trapper had closed his cabin door against the deepening gloom of the woods, lighted his coal-oil lamp, and started a cheery fire, the wolverine drew back into the enveloping darkness of the forest.

At the first glimmer of dawn he emerged from his improvised den and sought his breakfast where he knew it could most easily be obtained, to wit, on one of the traplines that had engrossed his wicked attention for so many opulent days. A close scrutiny of the trail with eye and nose, and a careful reconnoitering of the cabin, told him that the venture was safe. A weasel in its winter ermine, held in the first trap, occupied him for a few brief minutes, but he was too fastidious to break his fast on such stringy and musty meat when better could doubtless be found. After he had torn the distant cousin of his tribe from the steel jaws and mangled it, he proceeded up the line, and had not gone far when he sniffed the delicious odor of frozen fish.

It lay in broken bits upon the smooth surface of the snow, and the wolverine knew from past experience what this portended. He studied the layout with comprehending, savage eyes. Circling the baited area, he snatched at the outermost pieces and gulped them down. This was a breakfast much to his liking, and he craved the larger chunks that lay at the center. But his unerring instinct warned him that danger lurked beneath so tempting a feast, and that the utmost circumspection was needed to obtain it without imperiling his freedom.

With the nicest caution, he advanced upon the flavory morsels, placing his feet with slow deliberation and sniffing the snow inquiringly. Suddenly he paused, for the tell-tale odor of iron came up to his nostrils through the powdery whiteness. He stretched out a paw and delicately scraped away the snow until the trap lay exposed, then bared his teeth in a snarl and sat back upon his haunches to gloat over the unmasked fraud.

As he did so, he shot into the air with an appalling screech, blended of fury and fear. Half doubling upon himself in mid-jump, and alighting with savage claws unsheathed, he tore frantically with his forepaws at a clinging, biting thing of steel that had seized upon his short, hairy tail with a grip as cruel as that of his own jaws. For the trapper cunningly had supplemented his main set with a second trap, which he had washed in lye and held in a smudge to destroy the scent of iron and human hands, and handled with gloves treated in the same manner. With infinite care to preserve the unsullied appearance of the snow surface, he had placed it where he thought the robber would stumble into it while engrossed in his designs upon the center trap. But it had hardly occurred to him that the animal would sit down upon it!

Writhing and springing about in his mad endeavors to free himself of the horrible appendage, the creature continued to claw wildly at the trap, and again and again seized it with his teeth and tried to crush it between his powerful jaws. But the awful thing clung despite his efforts, and bit into the bone of his tail the harder.

Real fear entered the heart of the wolverine for perhaps the first time in its dauntless career. An impulse to flee to the familiar refuge, to which so cumbersome a thing as a trap could not be expected to follow, was acted upon with suddenness, and the animal gave a mighty bound toward the trunk of an adjacent tree. As the chain tautened against the heavy clog, the trap was arrested in midair with a jerk that mere hair and skin could not survive, and the covering of the tail gave and slipped smoothly from the bone. The wolverine sprawled to the snow, released from the agonizing clutch, but at the expense of a smarting tail stump.

He turned and snarled ragefully at the fearsome thing that had torn him with its teeth and was so indifferent to his own, and backed slowly off, terror still possessing him. His appetite for frozen fish was gone, and his arrogant assurance flown. He wanted nothing so much as to get away from the scene of his humiliation and pain, and to seek a shelter where he could curl up and nurse his wound.

And his desire was heightened by the sound of gliding snowshoes that suddenly traveled to his ears on the thin, frosty air. His glowering eyes shifted down the trail, and into them flamed an unquenchable hatred for the approaching master of the trap; then he turned reluctantly and stole silently away into the forest.

Gabe viewed the evidence of the wolverine's experience with both satisfaction and regret. The bunch of fur in the jaws of the trap made plain to him what had occurred.

"Put yer tail into it that time, didn't ye!" he chuckled, vastly pleased at the partial success of his stratagem. "Wish to blazes ye'd put her foot into it instead, yer thievin' varmint; there'd be one less glutton in the woods to steal furs. Reckon that skinned tail o' yourn's givin' ye somethin' to think about, though, an' mebbe ye'll keep away from my traps fer a spell."

Gabe's elation over having outwitted the wiliest of the forest dwellers increased as several days passed without further signs of the animal. Apparently the fright and pain of its experience had caused it to withdraw from the field, and he congratulated himself upon the outcome. His catch of fur increased gratifyingly, and, if the take continued, the accumulation of skins in his shed by Christmastime would make a sizable bale for packing into the settlement.

But the wolverine had not left the vicinity of the forks of the Swiftwater. Chastened, but sullen, he kept to his old haunts, giving the traplines, however, a wide berth. His temper, always of a surly, ungovernable quality was, if possible, made more undependable by the annoyance of a tail sensitive to the slightest friction. Therefore, when, about a week after the frozen fish had lured him to his undoing, he drifted across the zigzag trail of an animal dragging a trap and its hindering clog through the snow, he failed to be warned by the odor of wolf in the tracks and followed them in savage mood.

A lone timber wolf, a pariah from some pack ranging the coverts for grouse or rabbits, had stepped into an unbaited trap set for lynx near a rabbit runway, and its strength had enabled it to drag the heavy clog a long distance from the spot. When the wolverine drew near to the grizzled gray captive, whose plunging efforts to advance seemed in some way retarded, his shrewd eyes saw that the clog had become wedged between two close-growing saplings. Thereupon he climbed a tree and traveled from limb to limb to a point directly over the wolf, which now became aware that it was being stalked.

Descending well beyond range of the reaching jaws, the wolverine crept slowly and cautiously toward the harassed brute. The pain of the biting steel, intensified by its mad straining to advance, and the arrogant attitude of the wolverine, drove the wolf into a paraoxysm of fury. But strain as it would, it could not reach the tantalizing little beast that confronted it with such impudent calm.

Suddenly the wolverine darted in and raked a claw-studded paw across the face of his victim. The immense power of his forearm was in the slashing stroke, which laid bare the right cheek of the wolf and half blinded one eye.

And then it seemed as if retribution was to visit the insolent little scourge of the woods, for, at the instant following the wolverine's attack, the wolf had at last won free from the trap and launched itself upon its adversary, crushing him into the snow with the violence of its attack.

The surprised trouble-seeker quickly awoke to his peril and brought all his wit and cunning into play. He would have retreated if he could, for he knew himself to be outclassed in a fair fight with a full-grown wolf; but he was given no opportunity to flee, for his foe had him down and was worrying him cruelly, its punishing jaws searching for a hold on the black throat. The wolverine luckily succeeded in wriggling over on his back, the better to bring his sabrelike claws into play, and he raked the wolf with slashes that no living thing could long endure.

The fresh strength of the chunky little animal gave him an advantage over the larger and heavier beast, for the wolf's staying powers had been sapped by its long struggle with the trap. Also, its injuries were telling upon it, and it was further handicapped by its semi-blindness on one side. Had it not been for these factors, the result of the wolverine's temerity would doubtless have been fatal to him; but luck favored him, for the wolf's vitality was ebbing fast, while his own was scarcely impaired. He was wounded in many places by the sharp, rending teeth on which the wolf mainly depended for offense, but had managed, by shrinking his upper body into a compact mass, to evade the seizure of his throat, the coarse, thick fur making a grip there difficult to obtain; while throughout the struggle his own terrible weapons had been desperately employed.

Inferior in stamina to the wolverine through the force of circumstances, the wolf's chances were appreciably waning. As the vigor of its efforts subsided, the other redoubled his exertions, and, taking advantage of a second's cessation in the enemy's onslaught, twisted violently from his position and regained his feet. The wolf sprang to recover its advantage, but the wolverine was quicker. At last the gray-furred form sank into the snow, the victim of its smaller, but relentless, foe.

The gashes that covered the wolverine were distressingly evident, however, now that the lust for battle was sated, and his racked body craved shelter where he could lie and lick his wounds. He dragged himself painfully to a fissure high up in a ledge of rock a short distance off, and there remained for nearly a week.

Meanwhile, Gabe had discovered that his blind set had been sprung, and trap and clog carried away by an animal that had not figured in his plans. He followed the plain trail of the wolf, and, coming upon its torn body, read in that evidence the story of the wolverine's exploit.

"Blamed if the little cuss ain't still hangin' round and sp'ilin my furs!" he grumbled, in a mixture of disgust and admiration. "He's sure a gritty little critter to tackle a wolf, even if it was ketched in a trap. Looks like somethin' happened that he had n't figgered on, though, an' I reckon it was only his smartness that got him off."

Gabe surmised that the victor had holed up to recover from its wounds, and he followed the wolverine's blood-marked trail to the base of the ledge, but, on reaching it, realized that no human could scale its face. Grinning ruefully at this checkmate, he returned to the trapline, his feeling of assurance over the future gone.

When the wolverine's hurts were fully mended and his old-time arrogance had returned to him, his restored body craved stronger food than had sustained him during his healing; and on happening across a deer trail one morning, his hunger for venison became overpowering.

Selecting a leaning tree, a branch from which overhung the trail, he ascended it and crawled out along the limb, flattening himself upon it above the runway. Here he remained for hours in absolute immobility, except for his roving eyes which peered expectantly up and down the approaches.

Not until the sun was high in the cloudless winter sky and the wolverine's hunger nearly past endurance was his patience rewarded. A fine, antlered buck came stepping down the trail, quivering nostrils alert for the smell of danger, but all unwarned of the crouching terror that awaited him, for the wolverine's scent did not fall to the lower level of air. As the buck passed below the limb, the black form fell like a stone upon its back. The deer snorted with terror and pain, and then bounded into the air in a series of plunges that would have shaken off a less determined rider. Next he darted in among the trees, striving to scrape off the clinging horror; but, unsuccessful in this and crazed with fear, returned to the familiar trail, down which he raced with panic-stricken leaps.

Now it chanced that the trapper's supply of fresh meat had run low, and he had selected this same day in which to restock his larder with venison. With his rifle, he was still-hunting a cleft in a hardwood ridge when the sound of a flying deer came to his hearing. He awaited its approach with weapon ready for a snap-shot, and wondered what pursuing enemy it was that drove it at such speed. As the rocketing animal flashed across his vision, he fired, aware at the instant that the enemy was not pursuing, but was aboard. The deer faltered at the shot, plunged on for a few broken strides, and fell sprawling in the snow, shot through the heart. Gabe ran forward, and was amazed and elated as he saw the wolverine slip from the back of the deer and glide off into the brush. He fired at the vanishing black shape, but too late. Nevertheless, he sent an exultant shot after the vanquished fellow hunter.

"Drive a deer up to me, will ye, when ye knew I was sp'ilin' fer a haunch o' venison!" he taunted. "Well, ye're a fergivin' little cuss, an' this squares ye fer clawin' up a prime wolf pelt fer me. I've got the meat, whether ye meant it fer me or no, and I'm thankful to ye."

The buck was full grown and too heavy to be carried whole to the cabin, and Gabe concluded to make two loads of it. He skinned and dressed it and divided the carcass. The fore part he carried some distance off the trail and hung by the antlers in the fork of a tree limb. Making a sling of the skin, in which he wrapped the other half, he threw this over his shoulder and started for the camp, certain that the wolverine's fear of the rifle shots would drive it afar and prevent its return to the spot for at least a few hours.

But Gabe reckoned without the animal's growing disdain for a human who seemed impotent actually to harm it.

Quietly it slunk back to the scene and drew near while Gabe was still engaged with the carcass, with bared teeth snarling soundlessly at the irritating spectacle.

When Gabe shouldered his burden and departed, the wolverine advanced cautiously and followed him for a short distance, then returned and ranged warily about the spot, suspicious to a trap. Coming up beneath the hanging forequarters of the deer, it studied the ground and tree with minute scrutiny for many minutes. Finally its voracity conquered, the appetizing smell of fresh venison overpowering its prudence. It could not reach the meat from below, and climbed the tree to try to dislodge the wedged antlers.

Biting and clawing savagely at the antlers in its impatience, the wolverine failed to note the trapper's return until it was startled by the close sound of his approach and instantly slunk away into the shadows.

"I'll leave ye hungry this time, I reckon," Gabe muttered vindictively. "I've got the whip-hand of ye for once, an' not a bite o' the deer will ye get."

The wolverine soon was back at its old pastime of interference with the traps, and only by the exercise of sharpened ingenuity could Gabe achieve a reasonable catch. He shortened the old lines and laid new ones; and as the robber could not be in all places at one time, the trapper gathered a modest harvest of furs.

A week before Christmas Gabe decided that he would not brave the gibes of the settlement folk by exhibiting his small catch and explaining the cause. He would await the breaking up of winter to take his furs in, and trust to a large measure of success during the coming months—perhaps with the marauder disposed of.

He had dwelt vaguely at times on the advisability of shifting his base to a trapping ground higher up on the West Branch; and he thought to make a casual view of this section an excuse for a brief absence. As soon as he determined upon this he made up a small pack, banked his fire, and, shutting his cabin tight against intruders, set forth with ax and rifle for the upper waters of the Branch.

The wolverine marked his going, and trailed him curiously to the boundaries of the grounds. There it lay watchfully for a time, then slouched back to the traps and pursued its usual tactics along the line. It drew near to the clearing at dusk and peered from the wall of trees at the cabin, which seemed deserted. The trapper did not appear by nightfall, and the wolverine lingered at its post far into the night in vague puzzlement.

In the early dawn of the morning it again studied the camp. Clearly the man had not returned. Its keen nose, vastly more dependable than its full-sighted eyes, could catch no human scent. It circled the clearing, but discovered no fresh tracks, and little by little drew closer to the cabin.

The wolverine searched for an entrance, sniffing and scratching at the door and along its base at front and back, the sides being obstructed by the trapper's stacked supply of firewood. A tiny window high up on one side of the cabin was protected by a stout slab shutter which resisted its efforts to tear it loose. The wolverine had climbed to it on the pile of wood, and from there it was an easy jump to the peaked roof.

At last its attention was drawn to the chimney of stone and clay, and this provided an easy way in. It slipped quickly down the rough interior. At the bottom a sheet of tin gave instantly to its weight, and, springing clear of the heap of hot ashes in the fireplace, it was in the cabin.

The larder first attracted it, and it reveled in Gabe's supplies of salt pork, flour, molasses, and dried apples, breaking into the sacks and pails gleefully, and stuffing its rapacious stomach nearly to bursting. Then, with the abandon of a mischievous monkey loosed in a toyshop, it began its career of ruin throughout the cabin. Gabe's bunk was despoiled of its balsam mattress and the tips scattered over the floor; every article of bedding and clothing was torn into shreds, moccasins chewed into a pulpy mass, and spare snowshoes denuded of their webs. A high shelf drew its attention, and, in clutching at what it held, it pulled over on itself a tin of coal oil, drenching itself with the contents. The evil-smelling fluid was annoying, and it scrubbed its fur against the log walls and wallowed in the litter that covered the floor; but the odorous stuff still clung tenaciously.

At this moment it was startled into an attitude of strained hearing by a faint, familiar sound that caused its fur to bristle in anger and fear.

At a point only a little beyond the boundaries of his lines Gabe had camped for the night, and in the early morning had repented of his neglect of his duties for a cruise of which there was no vital need. So he hurried back, regretting the weakness that had prompted him to leave.

In a panic the wolverine leaped for the chimney as Gabe neared the hut. But, unaccountably, the tin sheet that had given way so easily when it entered, now became a smooth, inexorable barrier. The closed damper played the part of a trap-door.

When the wolverine sprang confidently for the opening, it was repulsed by the tin obstruction and fell sprawling into the heap of ash-covered coals in the fireplace. Scattered by its fall, and fanned into flickering life by the violence of its movements, the embers instantly ignited the oil-soaked fur of the animal. Enveloped in flames and squealing pitiably, it rushed about the cabin, leaving a blazing trail in the debris that it had so effectively prepared for its work of arson.

The weird sounds that came from the cabin as Gabe reached the entrance moved him to lift the latch without the delay of removing his snowshoes. As he opened the door, he was driven back in horrified wonder as a blast of flame and smoke smote him in the face. And at the same instant an animated streak of fire dashed between his legs, nearly upsetting him, and madly circled about in the snow.

The trapper raised his rifle and ended the beast's suffering, then turned his attention to the cabin, which he saw could not be saved, nor anything it contained. He rushed around to the rear, where his fur shed joined it, and discovered to his relief that it had not yet been reached by the flames. Kicking off his snowshoes and entering, he salvaged his precious skins before the fire reached the structure.

He went around the still blazing logs and stood over the remains of what had been his arch tormentor for so long a period. Turning the body over with his foot he examined its tail. The tip was a bald knob of skin-covered bone.

"It's sure enough me old friend," Gabe addressed the stark form. "There wouldn't have been room fer another like ye on Swiftwater Forks, that's sartin. Ye're past further devilment, which is where I've wanted ye this long time; but the honors ain't with me, fer ye're dead through no wit o' mine, an' ye sure had yer innings with me afore ye went. I'm regretful ye had to go in such pain.

" 'T'is you that got the last lick, ye obstinate little blackleg, fer ye've drove me off the grounds; an' ye willed I'd go in to the Christmas doin's at the post, whether I would or no!" and he set out to gather his traps and snare wires.

Later in the day, drawing a crudely wrought sledge of poles fastened together with wire, on which was bound his all too small bundle of furs, the trapper started on the long and toilsome march to the settlement.

* * * * *

"The Feud on Swiftwater," by William Gerard Chapman. Published in St. Nicholas, *March 1919. Original text owned by Joe Wheeler. William Gerard Chapman wrote nature stories for popular magazines during the first third of the twentieth century.*

SCOUT WOLF-FIGHTER

Ladd Plumley

It all seemed so hopeless—even foolhardy—to remain there with his incapacitated Indian guide, when by getting away he could at least save his own life.
And every hour, during the bitterly cold nights, the wolves came closer.

* * * * *

Glen Opdycke was in the bow of the canoe which was a half mile behind that which held his uncle. Obie, a young Indian guide, a youth about the age of Glen, had been given charge of the canoe at the rear. With his paddle he was skillfully directing a course through one of the most dangerous of the rapids of the Matisgum, a large river which flows toward Hudson Bay in the province of Quebec, Canada.

Before the canoe and on both sides stretched seething water, with sharp rocks here and there amid the boiling rapids. Just as the young Indian was using his utmost strength in keeping the canoe away from the whitewater and in the channel, suddenly the paddle blade broke short off, leaving in Obie's hand but a three-foot bit of splintered spruce.

Glen saw the accident, instantly reaching for the second paddle, which lay in the bottom of the canoe, intending to pass it to Obie; but he was not quick enough. With a side lurch, the craft swung out of the channel and shot her nose fairly into a sharp, projecting rock, the canoe splitting into two sections backward for several feet from the bow, as if the tough birch bark had been paper and were slit by a hunting knife.

For the next twenty minutes, Glen knew only a confused medley of frenzied thoughts, which surged through his mind as he attempted to save his life, battling in the grip of the fierce current. Under ordinary circumstances he was a good swimmer; but amid the icy, watery tumult, and in the grasp of the many crosscurrents, his swimming powers, without the aid of another, would have been of no avail. He was tossed here and there like a drowning insect in a mill sluice. In the midst of the spume of an eddy, as he was sucked under the surface, he would close his mouth, and it would seem to him that his lungs were bursting. A few moments later his head would be tossed upward, and, fighting desperately, he would gain a little air. But once more he was sucked downward, with a grip on his body that was impossible to withstand, and another seemingly endless period passed before he was flung upward and could once more gulp another breath of air.

Then, as if he heard the words from an immense distance, over the rush and boom of the rapids came, "Grab hold and hold fast!" and he became conscious he had something within his grasp, something that he found later was the handle of Obie's broken paddle.

After he had seized the bit of spruce, it seemed that another endless time passed before he knew he was in smooth water near the shore and that Obie was shouting something in French, which he could not understand. Some minutes later he lay stretched out on the rocks of the shore. The voice of the booming rapids seemed to be booming within his head, but the sunshine was so warm, so warm! And it was so good to breathe air and breathe easily—so good! And he knew Obie was looking down at him with a smile on his face, and the Indian was not given to smiling.

In excellent English, for Obie has been to school in Quebec, he exclaimed, "Good! The wicked red river-devils—the red river-devils, they did not get you! They wanted you bad, the red river-devils, but they did not get you this time!"

"If it hadn't been for you!" gasped Glen. "If it hadn't been for you!" He shuddered, turning his eyes aside from the tossing rapids in front of him.

"We should make a fire!" growled Obie, turning away, Indianlike hating praise. "A fire! But—how?"

Glen fumbled in his khakis, producing a waterproof match safe, which he held out. "I always carry dry matches," he said. "Before my uncle brought me along on the fishing trip, I tried out that match safe in a pail of water. It's all right!"

"Good!" grunted the Indian. "My bottle of matches is out somewhere in the river!"

Soon both were drying themselves beside a hot fire, the Indian keeping well away from his young master, and now as silent as he had always been since the fishing party had left civilization behind them. But Glen talked. It seemed so good to be sitting beside a fire and listening to the angry voice of the river, but knowing you were safe. Yes, Glen talked. He thanked the young Indian; he praised his presence of mind in keeping his grip on the bit of spruce to which Glen owed his life—or, rather, the bit of spruce with which the Indian had saved him. He heaped praises on silent Obie, who from time to time shrugged his shoulders as if throwing off the thanks of the young American. "I'm a Boy Scout," went on Glen. "Do you know what a scout is?"

"In the school in Quebec I have heard talk of Boy Scouts," grunted the Indian. "They live in cities, but they make fire as my people once did. That is a fine thing. People should not forget forest ways. That is what my father says: 'Forget not the forest ways,' he says. 'Many moons ago, all men of the earth were like the Indians— they were all forest men and knew forest ways, and it is good to remember forest ways even when men live in big cities.' "

"Boy Scouts," went on Glen, "they do good turns when they can; but your good turn—I can never repay you—never!"

The Indian shrugged his shoulders once more. "We must dry ourselves before we try to find your uncle and my father. And while we dry ourselves, I will talk a little. And we in Canada, many of us are guides, guides and hunters and trappers. My father in winter is a trapper for the Hudson's Bay Company, and he is a guide in summer. All my folks are guides and trappers. A guide is different from other men. And our fathers teach us when we are kids, as you Americans call little boys. Long ago my father tells me a story—a story of his father, my grandfather. We must get dry, and while we wait I will tell you the story.

"My grandfather is in the spirit land," went on Obie. "But when he was here, everybody, in Quebec and in cities in the States, those who came hunting and fishing, they knew he was a fine brave guide.

"Once my grandfather was guiding some Englishmen on a salmon river, a river down on the Labrador coast; and there was another guide; and my grandfather thought bad of the other guide. The other guide was very proud and he was very foolish and his name was Tamon.

" 'Get out the canoe, Tamon!' said one of the Englishmen. 'I go and fish the river!' But my grandfather tells how dangerous the river is, for it is high with rain and flood. But the Englishman, he laughs. 'You are afraid!' he says to my grandfather. 'Not to go out on the river alone,' says my grandfather. 'No, I am not afraid of that! But I am afraid to take another. For if the canoe is overturned, then I must not leave my man, for I am a guide, and today the red river-devils would get us both!'

"But out into the river the Englishman and Tamon, they go. And the canoe is upset, and Tamon, he is a fine swimmer—he leaves his man and he swims toward the shore. But my grandfather, he runs and he gets his rifle and he shouts to Tamon to go back to his man. But Tamon keeps on right toward the shore, and the rifle goes off, and Tamon is shot! But the Englishman has sunk already and nothing can be done. So the red river-devils got the Englishman and the bad guide Tamon. This is a true story of my grandfather and the bad guide. And maybe it is not only once that things like that have come to bad guides. And when I was a little boy, my father tells me what a wicked thing is it not to stay by your man. And it is our life here—to take care of those who come to fish and hunt. And if we did not learn that we must never leave our man, then we should be like Tamon and be bad guides and deserve to be shot."

The other and much larger canoe, which carried the provisions and Glen's uncle and Obie's father, the well-known guide and trapper Samson, as he is called, was far in advance, and, of course, the accident to the following canoe was not known. But Obie believed there would be no great difficulty in following the riverbank and overtaking the others of the party. And Obie knew that when the following canoe did not appear, Samson would make a landing and together with Glen's uncle would begin a search for the missing boys.

Obie led the way down the river, but the route proved far more difficult than he had supposed. The river was new to him, and, indeed, he was acting as a guide for the first time in his life. At times, and very frequently, it was necessary to make wide detours from the water, for precipitous rocks overhung the river in places, over which the shoreline could not be followed.

As was learned much later, Obie's father waited for his son at the bottom of a particularly dangerous series of rapids. Not seeing the other canoe, Samson made a landing, and at once a search began. Unfortunately, however, the landing was made on the opposite side of the river from that on which Glen and Obie were meeting the difficulties of their journey. And it must have been when one of the necessary detours was made that the two parties passed each other on opposite sides of the river. Unfortunately, too, the crushed canoe swung to the other side, where it was seen by Samson, overturned and circling in an eddy. Hence, Obie's father and Glen's uncle believed that son and nephew lost their lives in the heavy rapids just above where the crushed canoe was seen. And upstream—not searching for the living, but for bodies of the dead—Mr. Opdycke and Samson continued their sad hunt.

On the opposite side, worn with scrambling over ledges and following the rock-encumbered shore, the travelers at sundown came to rest at the base of one of the walls of rock that overhung the river.

"You stay here!" grunted Obie. "I will climb the side of the rock, go around, and see if I can find the camping place. I think my father would go this far. You are tired—you stay here. If I find the camp, I will get food and come back. I go alone. You are what the Americans say, 'all in.' "

"I *am* pretty much all in," replied Glen. "I'll be glad to sit down. And hungry! Say, I think I could eat a raw trout!"

Glen sank upon a bit of sand, so completely exhausted that shortly he was fast asleep. But he did not sleep long, his desire to know if Obie had found the camp awakening him. He rose and paced back and forth on the bit of beach, waiting impatiently for Obie's return. As he continued to move about restlessly, he was conscious that over the booming of the rapids he heard a distant shout.

By this time it was night, but the sky was clear and the stars gave considerable light. In reply to the distant shout, Glen shouted again and again, thinking that Obie had found the camp and was shouting the news on his return trip. But the shouts were constantly repeated; and as they did not increase in loudness, it seemed evident that, if Obie were shouting, he was staying in the same place.

"This is a frightfully rough country to tramp over," said Glen, to himself. "Perhaps Obie has hurt himself. Guess I'd better hunt him up."

He scrambled over the rough broken ledges and away from the river and, guided by the shouts, which were constantly repeated, and which he as constantly answered, his progress was at length stopped by the route he was following seeming to drop over a considerable precipice, which, in the starlight, looked like a gulf of blackness.

"Go around—to the south!" came up a quavering yell from below.

Carefully Glen edged along the lip of the precipice until he found a kind of natural rock stairway, which, using great care, he managed to descend. Before long he was standing at the side of Obie, a dim figure sitting on the ground, just at the base of the rocky wall.

"You are hurt?" gasped Glen.

"Very bad!" grunted the Indian. "That is always the way! My people, they say, 'Bad things, they ever travel like the geese, always in flocks!' And I am to blame—very careless! I think I come down that rock all right, but it's rotten rock. A piece fell, and I fell. My leg! Ugh! It is very bad. The bone is smashed!"

At once Glen turned his attention to making a fire, for he wanted light to see how badly Obie was hurt. When he had thrown dry twigs on the fire and the glare lighted up the place, an examination proved that Obie was correct and that one of the bones of the left leg was broken between the ankle and the knee.

"If I don't do something to that leg, Obie, very likely you will always be lame, even if worse doesn't happen," said Glen. "I was taught by a doctor in Chicago how to set a broken leg. We scouts learn all sorts of things. I'm afraid I'll hurt you a lot, but I'll be as careful as I can. First I've got to have some splints—thin pieces of strong wood, you know!"

Obie pulled from his belt a hunting knife. "I always keep my knife sharp," he said. "Beyond the fire is a little spruce, winter killed. You can break it down and split it with my knife. A stone makes a good hammer for splitting wood with a knife. The spruce will make fine strong splinters."

When Glen had split out several stout splints and shaped them with the knife, Obie removed his cotton shirt and Glen slit it into strips. Then he cautiously handled the wounded leg, running his fingers back and forth until he found the place of the fracture.

"Now I must hurt you and hurt you bad," warned Glen. "I've got to pull out the leg so that the end of the broken bone will slip into place."

"Go ahead," growled Obie.

And although he must have suffered much while Glen was completing his work, he did not utter more than low groans. Glen had been taught by the doctor to stretch the leg until he felt that the bone had been pulled into position. This was his first job as a surgeon, and he found it very trying to his nerves. But at last the leg was wrapped in the splints, and a little later the Indian seemed more comfortable. "And now sleep!" said Obie.

Glen stretched himself beside Obie, and almost the next moment he was fast asleep; but the groans of his companion awakened him long before morning. The fire had burned down, and from far away in the forest came a howling—very distant and very faint, but clearly to be heard.

"What kind of animals make those howls?" asked Glen.

"Wolves!" replied Obie. "You'd better put wood on the fire. The wolves will not come near if we have a good fire!"

Glen groped about in the darkness, succeeding in finding some fallen branches, which he put on the coals. For some time he continued to listen to the distant howls, then he knew nothing until morning had come and the sunlight was streaming on his face.

The first thing was to get Obie some water, for fever had set in and he was thirsty. High ledges of rock were between the boys and the shore, but at a little distance Glen found a trickle of spring water. Obie told him how to peel a young canoe birch, and, with the bark, Obie constructed a rough but serviceable pail with which Glen brought water.

"What is best for me to do, Obie?" asked Glen, when his companion had satisfied his thirst.

"I did not sleep much, and I have been thinking of that," replied the Indian. "Your uncle and my father, they will find the broken canoe, and they will think the red river-devils got us. But they will not be sure, and they will hunt for us. So you must go to the river and make a big fire, and perhaps they will see the smoke. And you must tie something white to a pole, so it can be seen. But the river is wide and this is a big country. Many high rocks. They may go along the other side and never see those things. And, you see, they cannot get the canoe back up the rapids. And if they were on this side, they might never find us. We have no food. Soon we will be weak, and the leg makes me feel sick. So you must not wait. You must travel down the river. The settlements begin below. If you keep near the river, you will not get lost and you will make the settlements before you are too weak to walk. That is what you must do."

"And leave you here by your lonesome?"

"Yes."

"But the wolves might get you."

"You will pile up a pile of wood. And you will come back, or my father will see the smoke or the white on the pole, and he will find me."

"Say, suppose I were you? Had a broken leg? What would you do?"

"That is different. I am your guide."

"But what would you do?"

For some moments the Indian considered the matter, then he growled, "That is most different; but if you had the broken leg, this would I do: I would make the fire and tie the rag on the pole, and I would lay branches on the ground—spruce branches, with the little ends pointing down the river. If my father found them, he would know how we traveled. Then I should cut sapling crutches; and where I could not carry you, then you would use the crutches."

"You wouldn't leave me?"

"Never!" grunted the Indian.

"And do you really suppose that after you've saved me from your 'red river-devils' I'd leave you and get to the settlements alone? Say, what do you take me for?"

The Indian broke into a tirade of expostulations, but Glen silenced him with a gruff, "Cut it out! We'll be hungry together, and if you get so weak you cannot use crutches, I shall carry you. If the wolves have a feast, they'll have a double feast! I'm through talking. I'll get busy with the fire, the rag, and the crutches."

It was most unfortunate that the accident to Obie happened at the place where it did, for, in their search, Mr. Opdycke and Samson, back in the forest, must have been circling the place where the boys were at the time this conversation took place. At least that is the only way to explain that the boys were left behind and that the signals were never seen. For after an up-river search, Mr. Opdycke and Samson returned to their canoe, crossed the river, and, after a search on that side—which was difficult because of gulches and rocks—started for the settlements below for helpers, intending to return in the hope of recovering the bodies.

Beyond the middle of the second day, Glen has never been able to recall with distinctness all the details of that terrible journey. In many places precipitous banks were found. Constantly detours had to be made, and a mile of progress meant sometimes three miles or more of difficult travel.

Obie was not a lightweight, but, weakened as he was and ill with the fever brought on by his injury, Glen at times found it necessary to carry him, and to make the trip twice in order to return for the sapling crutches. Constantly Obie tried to dissuade him from these efforts, urging Glen to leave him and gain the settlements before it was too late. But Glen would clench his teeth, and, in a nightmare of effort, struggle onward, gasping, "Leave you, old fellow? You've got another guess coming!"

Then came a night when a storm was brewing and it was very dark. Wolves were now constantly trailing the boys; perhaps their acute animal wits told them that the time for an attack would soon come. Glen had become so weak that, although he exerted himself to his limit, on this night he could gather but a paltry heap of fallen branches and drift from near the river. He used his fuel sparingly, but long before morning only a few dry spruce branches were left.

The night before, the wolves had come close to the camping place, and on this night growlings and snappings were heard in the darkness, just beyond the circle of light made by the fire. Glen would sit on the ground, dozing, for he was exhausted almost to insensibility, and lack of food had reduced his strength so that on the day's march he had been able to aid his companion but little. Weakened by his fever and lack of nourishment, the Indian was oblivious to the peril which growled in the brush or at times broke out into yelpings. He lay upon the ground near the fire and knew nothing.

As the flames sank lower, the circle of white-fanged death in the blackness closed in on the boys. Dimly Glen recognized that this night the wolves intended an actual attack, and he restrained himself from using his last fuel, reserving it against the moment of greatest need. At times he relapsed into unconsciousness; then he would find himself awake; and from the brush would come the footfalls of padded feet, the snapping of twigs, and low growls.

Suddenly came a savage yelp, as one of the wolves, doubtless the leader of the pack, leaped from the brush and was almost upon the unconscious Indian before Glen could light one of his spruce branches in the coals of the fire.

The boy was not the fraction of a second too soon. Waving the lighted branch, he turned to face, in the glow of his torch, a gaunt, grim creature, its lips curled back, its mouth dripping white froth, and its red eyes glinting fury.

With a gasping yell, Glen staggered toward the gray terror. But the wolf did not retreat until the lighted branch actually touched its shaggy head, then it slipped back into the darkness; but its red eyes—and other red eyes—told that the retreat was only a feint and that soon another attack would be made.

The bit of dry spruce branch has scarcely burned out to blackness, when it came. And again and again, as the brand flickered out, a new attack would be made, either by the leader of the pack or by one of the other wolves. The hours of frenzied fighting reduced Glen almost to actual madness. And no wonder! Gasping his cries, he would grope in the dark for another bit of branch. Then, in the gleam of his petty torch, he would stagger between Obie and an attacking wolf. On and on wore the night, and he never knew when, at length, the faint white light of a dull dawn came over the forest to the east, and the disappointed leader of the pack gave growling orders for a retreat.

The light trembled downward amid the trees; the wolves were far away; but the gasping protector of the unconscious Indian still staggered here and there with a charred and extinguished bit of spruce in his blackened and burned hand. Then he dropped to the ground, and, hours later, awakened to know that Obie was shaking him.

"The wolves! They are coming again! I hear them! See their eyes!" gasped Glen.

"It is day," said the Indian. "The wolves have gone. Last night I knew nothing. But there are tracks—an arm's stretch from where I was; and burned bits of brush all about. I know! But for you, the gray wood-devils would have made their kill!" After a moment he added: "I am weak, so weak I cannot go farther. But even yet you can get near the settlements where the wolves never go. Yes, that is the way. You must go!"

For some time Glen did not reply. Gradually he was overcoming the horror of his fight. But he heard Obie, and at last he answered: "Tonight the wolves will get us. I can never do what I did last night. Yes, the wolves will get us!" He shuddered and closed his eyes.

"No, you cannot fight the gray devils more," grunted the Indian. "But you have strength and you must go. You must travel fast."

Slowly Glen staggered to his feet. For a long time he looked his companion in the eyes. Then he spoke, pointing toward the river. "I don't know how you Indians would say what I want to say, but here's my way of putting it: if your father or my uncle doesn't get here in time and find us—and, as you say, you cannot go any farther—yes, the wolves will get us—tonight. Well, I shall leave you; leave the fellow who saved my life in the rapids! Yes, of course, I shall leave him to die alone! But that, Obie—and listen to me, listen!—that will only be when all the water out there in the river has run away and the bottom rocks are dry everywhere. That's my answer, old fellow!"

The Indian seemed to have been scarcely listening. He was gazing back into the forest, where the first light of a gloomy day obscured everything at a little distance. "You are young, but you are brave!" he said. "And as you have been talking your brave words, something back there in the mist, I know not what, but something has been talking, too; very low, but there are times when my people hear the forest voice, and I hear the forest voice. It is talking now, and it says that the gray devils of sharp teeth, the gray devils will not make their kill. This is what I hear! The voice tells me more. It says that you and I shall live for many years, and that the beasts and river-devils, they shall never have us. This is what I hear, and you shall find it is a true word!"

In his half-delirium from weakness and fever had the Indian been granted the tongue of prophecy? It would really seem so. That noon, in the heavy rain, for a storm had begun, sitting at the side of Obie, who had not been able to rise, Glen heard a distant shout. Both the Indian and Glen weakly replied, and a half-hour later Obie's father and Glen's uncle emerged from behind a mass of willows at the edge of the river.

A little later Glen found himself sitting beside a good fire, with a blanket wrapped around him, eating some hot soup. And never will soup taste to Glen as it did that day.

When the party arrived at the settlement, Obie received the attention of a doctor, who said that the young Indian would not be even slightly lame and that the broken bone had been set almost as neatly as a surgeon could have done it.

And when Glen returns to his home and his scout-patrol in Chicago, his fellow scouts will doubtless call him by a name different from the name by which they have known him hitherto, for in the village were five Indians, guides and winter trappers for the Hudson's Bay Company. The five represented the tribe of which Samson and Obie are the hereditary chieftains, and, at a solemn meeting, Glen was made one of the tribe's warriors, with all the ancient ceremonies usual on such an occasion. His ordinary American name was written on a sheet of bark and burned over a fire. Then the ashes were strewn to the four winds, and his Indian name, as a youthful chieftain of the tribe, was given to him: "Wolf-Fighter—the chieftain who, while the river runs, leaves not alone his red brother."

* * * * *

"Scout Wolf-Fighter," by Ladd Plumley. Published in St. Nicholas, *February 1921. Original text owned by Joe Wheeler. Ladd Plumley wrote for popular magazines during the first half of the twentieth century.*

THE WHITE TERROR
OF THE NORTH

Bernard Sexton

Fourteen-year-old Jack Anderson was left behind to watch over the dogs while the men went seal-hunting. "Ain't no bears around, I guess," were his father's parting words. Unfortunately, the boy had a visitor—a great white visitor.

* * * * *

"I guess this is a likely place for the snow house."

The speaker was Ole Anderson, a gigantic man with a good-natured red face which perpetually broke into a grin. He stopped the dogs and turned to the two men and the boy who followed the sled.

"It looks as good as any other place, Dad!" called out the boy, as he ran to the dogs and began unharnessing.

The two others said nothing, for they were men of few words, and the arctic wastes breed silence. They were Tom Henderson and his cousin Dick Hurley, both friends of Ole Anderson and his companions on many adventurous voyages. When Ole had left Seattle a month before in his little whaling ship, the *Happy Bird,* he had taken his fourteen-year-old boy with him on the trip, for, as he said, "Jack is almost as big as a man now, and why shouldn't he have a man's job when he wants it?" So to Jack's great delight, but with many misgivings on the part of his mother, he was allowed to go.

Ole had left the *Happy Bird* in a little sheltered harbor near Point Manning and had gone out on the ice with his son and his two companions to get seal. This was to be their first night camp on the ice. It was a thrilling moment for Jack when the dogs were unhitched and he realized that they were to stay on the ice and build a snow house like the Eskimos. Tom and Dick set to work immediately, cutting up the snow blocks for the igloo; and after Jack had watched them for a minute, he was able to help.

In an hour the house was built, and the ventilating hole, which was two or three inches in diameter, carefully bored in the top. Jack noticed that Tom and Dick took care to build the house on top of a deep drift, so that the snow actually insulated them from the cold of the ice underneath. To enter, they had to make their way along a passage, tunneled through the snow, and which led into the house by way of a hole in the floor. When Jack stood up inside, his head was a few inches below the roof.

By the time that Tom and Dick were beginning to unpack the sleds, Jack's father said to him, "I guess you can come with me for seal." And the two took their rifles from the pack and walked along until they came to the rough, hummocky ice that they had noticed ahead when they first made camp. On the way, Ole talked to Jack about the methods used in the capture of seal.

"The great thing," he said, "is to understand what the seal himself thinks. Now, up here on the arctic ice, the greatest enemy of the seal is the polar bear. The seal comes up and climbs out on the ice to get air and to sleep. On account of the danger from polar bears, he is careful never to sleep longer than a minute. Then he lifts his head and looks around. If he doesn't see anything looking like a polar bear, he puts his head down and sleeps for another minute, or even for thirty seconds. It's all right for the hunter to walk toward the seal till he's within four hundred yards, for beyond that a seal's eyesight isn't good. At four hundred yards you must begin to stalk him, and that I'm going to show you how to do."

They were now about a mile from camp. Ole looked around very carefully, and after an exhaustive survey, he pointed out a black thing on the ice about a quarter of a mile away. "Now," he said, "you watch me, and I'll show you how to stalk seal."

"But, Dad," said Jack, puzzled, "why don't you shoot him from here? I know you can do it."

"I couldn't score a brain shot from here," answered Ole, "and any other kind of shot would lose the seal; for he lies on slippery ice, and the least quiver after death sends him down into the water. Once there, he is likely to float under the ice, where we couldn't get him."

Ole lay down on the ice and began to work his way toward the seal. Whenever the seal looked around, Ole lay perfectly still, waiting until the watchful beast put his head down again. However, when Ole got within two hundred yards of the victim, he adopted new tactics. Once in a while, as the seal looked at him, he would raise up his leg and make motions as if scratching himself; and as this was what the seal himself was doing all the time, it drove home to his brain the conviction that Ole was only another seal, and so quite harmless.

When Ole got within seventy-five yards, Jack heard a sharp report, and, after that, the seal put up its head no more. Jack, who always hated killing animals, felt a little sad as he saw the fine creature lying so still. A moment later he was running toward Ole, who was now leisurely approaching his prize. They tied a rope around it and then Ole dragged it to camp, where he handed it over to Tom, who knew well how to cut up the seal.

The weather had been growing colder during the day, and now, with the temperature thirty below, Jack was glad to get into the snow house. Dick was there cooking supper over the blue-flame kerosene stove. Jack was astonished to find how warm the shelter was. He found it perfectly comfortable to sit on the ledge of snow covered with fur, that ran around the base of the house. He talked to Dick about the day's experience.

"Tom and I hev been sayin' as how it might be well to hev your father and us walk to the north tomorrow and look for silver fox," said Dick.

Ole's head appeared in the opening just then, and he crawled in, followed by Tom, who brought some of the seal blubber. "Yes, I reckon, Dick, you're right," he said. "If we could leave the lad here to take care of the dogs, we could look for the fox."

"I'm not scared to stay, Dad," answered Jack. "I'll be glad to take care of the dogs."

Ole nodded, and they went on with the supper. The snow house became warmer and warmer. Jack wondered how it was that the walls didn't melt, and Dick explained that the cold, penetrating from the outside, kept the snow hard.

"The colder it is outside, the warmer you can keep it inside," he said.

The comfort of it all soon made Jack drowsy; and before he knew it, he was fast asleep, while the men smoked and made their plans for the morning's trip.

When he woke, Dick was cooking breakfast, and the heat of the stove made their cozy house so warm that they all sat up in their sleeping bags without any extra covering from the waist up. Then the men dressed and went outside to feed the dogs. Ole and the boy followed them in a few minutes.

"We're a little scarce on cartridges," said Ole, "but I'll leave you six for the rifle. All you got to do is to sit around and take care of things. If we ain't back till tomorrow, you can tie up the dogs tonight, and we'll be in in the morning early. Ain't no bears around here, I guess."

* * * * *

Jack found the hours of that day rather long and monotonous, and he was really glad when "night" came, and when, after feeding the dogs, he crawled into the snow house and made supper. Immediately thereafter he curled up in his sleeping bag and fell asleep.

Through his dreams, at last, he heard the staccato barking of the dogs, and by the way they spoke, he knew, with a jump of the heart, that a polar bear was approaching. Jack had lain down in his clothes. Now he hastily jumped out of the bag and seized the rifle. The savage frenzy of the dogs increased. For a moment Jack was very much afraid. He didn't want to go out and meet the chances of death—but he hesitated only for a moment. He knew that if he didn't go out, if he allowed his fear to master him, the dogs would be torn to pieces in a very few minutes.

When he emerged from the entrance it was light, and he saw the bear leisurely walking in the direction of camp. It was an enormous beast, and utterly fearless. Jack realized the truth of what his father had told him a few days before, that the bears in the far northern ice, many of whom have never seen man, are utterly unconscious of danger. Jack's first bullet seemed to miss the great beast, but he paused at the report with a puzzled look, and then came on with the same swinging stride as before. The second bullet hit him. He stopped for a few seconds and looked at Jack, as if doubting whether or not *he* was important. At that moment Jack, aiming for his head, fired for the third time. To his astonishment, the bear, instead of dropping to the ground, leaped ahead and charged!

Jack knew he had time for but one more shot and that he must not miss. The huge white creature that came bounding toward him was the most terrifying sight that he had ever seen. There was just one thing he wanted to do, and that was to throw down the rifle and run. But he controlled the impulse, and when the bear was only forty feet away, he fired once more.

And still the monster kept on coming! Then Jack threw down his weapon and turned to run. As he did so, he saw hurrying figures coming toward him. They were shouting. A second later he was flung violently to the ground, as the bear leaped upon him. His head hit the hard ice and he lost consciousness. As he fell, he seemed to hear from what seemed an enormous distance a small *pop, pop, pop*!

* * * * *

When Jack came to himself, he found he was lying in the snow house, and the men, with their grave, kind faces, were sitting around watching him. Ole was sitting by his side. He held in his hand a lump of ice with which he had been chafing the head of the boy. His face lighted up wonderfully when he saw Jack open his eyes.

"Well, Jack, my boy," he said, "you'll have something to talk of when you go back. You're the youngest lad that ever killed a polar bear, I guess."

Jack looked inquiringly from one to the other.

"Are you sure it was my bullets that killed him, Dad?" he asked. "It seemed to me that I missed all my shots and that I heard you firing as I fell. I guess it was you who killed him, after all," and he grinned at his father.

"Not a bit of it!" cried Ole. "I did fire three shots as he fell, but it was your bullets did the work—we found one in his heart. Now don't talk any more, son."

Tom and Dick nodded vigorously and always maintained that it was the "tad's" bullet that killed the big bear whose enormous skin, a week later, ornamented the cabin of the *Happy Bird*.

* * * * *

"The White Terror of the North," by Bernard Sexton. Published in St. Nicholas, *January 1921. Original text owned by Joe Wheeler. Bernard Sexton wrote for popular magazines during the first half of the twentieth century.*

THE BOY AND THE BEAST

Nora Burglon

From Norway comes this story of a boy's love for his pet—a wolf cub. But his uncle was determined to get rid of the wolf first chance he got.
Then that chance came.

* * * * *

"Evald!"

"Huh?"

"I need more birch bark. Trot yourself along and get me some more."

"Did you take what was in the old herring barrel?"

" 'Course!"

"Do I have to go 'way out into the woods to get it?" asked the boy timidly.

"Woods? Naturally! Where else?"

To be sure, that sounded simple enough, but in reality it was not at all simple, for Evald, as all of Norway, was afraid of the dark. The afternoon sun had scaled old Esfjallen and was going down the other side. That meant that it was already growing dark between the steep walls of the mountains.

"Well," interrupted the Farbro ["Father's brother": therefore, uncle], "what are you waiting for? Get started and hurry along!" With that he laid down his netting needle, for he was in the habit of talking with his hands.

"Can't I go tomorrow morning instead?"

"No!"

Since there was nothing to do about it, the boy started off. Evald ran as fast as he could, considering that the shoes he wore were of heavy wood and very clumsy. Had they not been such clogs that nobody else would wear them, Ole would surely have sold them to somebody for an öre or so.

A brown trail of tree girths blazed his way as he stole cautiously through the woods. Each of the larger trees wore a badge of brown where the knives of the fisher folk had ripped the bark away. A noble badge it was, too, for what would these poor sons of the sea have done without the supple bark of the birch groves! Woven sandals and shoes they gave; baskets and brooms and floats for the nets; paper to write upon; and they served as many other purposes as the ingenious one wished to put them to.

The Laplanders have dealt harshly with these old-timers, observed Evald, running his fingers over the brown gashes. *I thought they had left long since,* he continued, *but this was done not more than two days ago!* It was now the time of the year when the Laplanders took their herds to the mountains—or rather, the herds took them. Evald wished they had left some bark for him. But no, he had to go way in where it was thick with black shadows!

He knew the forest was no place for him once his mind began to play pranks with his imagination; so he hastily gathered up what bark he had, fitted the curling pieces within one another, and started for home. However, he did not get far before something arrested his attention. At first he thought it was a movement in the leaves, and then he thought it was a cry! He wanted to drop the bark and run for his life, but he dared not move! Stiff with fright, he stood there motionless and waited for the end to come. The Huldran [A female troll. All of Scandinavia was so frightened by tales of the supernatural, that old and young alike were terrified in the dark.] had surely come to get him this time!

Now! There she was! Out of the earth she was coming! Huldran! See! The leaves were rising! She was going to rise out of the earth and grab him! Evald watched the spot in terror and waited for the worst to come. But it was not the Huldran after all! It was a little woolly animal. Instantly Evald forgot his terror and fell to his knees. "It's a dog!" he cried, "A little woolly puppy!"

Never had the boy's voice vibrated with such undisguised joy before. All his life he had longed for something of his own—some living thing—but it had always been the same story! The Farbro had scarcely enough to feed Evald, not to mention another mouth to look after. But this was different. Surely the Farbro

could not refuse him this little fellow! He was so very small; he could not require much. It was not until then that the boy noticed how starved the creature looked. It appeared, indeed, as if the coat he was wearing was much too large for him, and quite without lining, for it lay in wrinkles over his ribs. There seemed to be nothing but bones under it, so poor was the little beast.

Evald put him into his shirt so that he could keep him warm with the heat from his own body, for the little thing was shivering and shaking as if half frozen.

Evald became stricken with a new fear. What if this little fellow should die of hunger before he could find him something to eat! He hastily gathered up the bark once more and ran through the forest with the most amazing speed. Over the rocks and the heather he went, nor did he think of either Neise or Huldran, troll or mountain demon!

He scrambled over the stile and dropped the bark. He left it lying where it fell, for Bjella was munching grass on the other side and it was she, of course, he was most interested in right then. "Come, Bossy, come," coaxed Evald, wiggling his forefinger at her. "Come and give this hungry one something to eat!" But Bjella was not interested. She gave Evald a disconcerted glance and kept right on in the direction she had set out for; she did not intend to be foster mother to anything. Cows were like that! They would never show any one respect unless they had to. Evald ran up to her, and taking her by the bell strap, gave it a jerk. She could understand that!

It did not take long for the boy to direct a stream into the nervous little mouth which drank the warm milk down with such amazing eagerness; Evald was surprised that one little fellow could hold so much. Bjella was actually so horrified at this hungry little beast that she lifted her legs and solemnly walked away; which was doubtless a very good thing, else the puppy would surely have put an end to himself. Evald stuck the animal back into his shirt, picked up the birch roll, and ran along home.

"Oy-yoy-yoy-yoy!" complained the Farbro, just as Evald had expected he would. "You keep on getting slower and slower ev-er-y day." Then he sighed painfully and took up the birch bark to inspect it. "I have been sitting here waiting for a whole hour," he continued. "What kept you so long this time? Can't you move those long pokar [legs] of yours?"

"The Laplanders have stripped all the trees where I used to go, so I had to go deep into the woods," explained Evald.

"Eh?" cried the Farbro, sharply. "Excusing again, always excusing!" With that he took out his sheath knife and commenced to work at the bark.

Evald wanted to get out of the hut, go anywhere just to get away before the Farbro should see how he stuck out in front, but he dared not leave before the Farbro told him to. Neither did he dare tell about finding the creature, for when Ole said, "oy-yoy-yoy-you," it meant that he was at the end of his patience. Just then, of all times and places, the puppy commenced to whimper!

"Eh?" cried the Farbro, "What are you standing there whimpering about?" He was angry now, so he did not pause to lift his glasses! "There is the cow shed to clean, and the horses to feed, and the chickens to care for, and the wood to split. Get yourself a-moving before you take root and grow in one place, for then, like as not, I shall have to take care of you the rest of your life!"

"Yes, Farbro," responded Evald dolefully, for he dared not let him know he was happy to be sent about these old tasks of his. That would never do.

"When you get through with that," added the Farbro after Evald's retreating figure, "clean out the henhouse, and then milk the cow. After that, set the kettle on the fire and make some milk porridge for supper tonight, for that is what I have my mind set on." Evald was now at the stable door, and so far away he did not deem it necessary to answer. "And hurry up!" called the Farbro, by way of ending up his orders.

The first thing Evald did was to get some of the fine yellow wool which hung in the hempen bag in the stable and put it into Bjella's winter feed box. "This is going to be your home, little fellow," he told the puppy, putting him down into the warm woolen nest. Then Evald skipped about and did his work up in a hurry. He fed the horse and the hens; next he took up the ax and split wood until the chips flew right and left. He filled the wood box and ran to the well to get a bucket of water. Then he ran down the lane to get the cow, and as he ran along, he whistled until the distant foothills caught up the echo and sent it back again, in the playful manner of mountain echoes.

"Oy-yoy-yoy-yoy!" cried Ole, as he heard the boy coming back with the cow, whistling as merrily as any culprit. "What can have gotten into Evald, he that goes about from morning until night with no more sound in him than a rooster with his head off! I must go and find out right now." So saying, he put down his book and his spectacles, and got up from his three-legged stool, groaning as he always did. He limped over to the door and leaned against the frame for a moment until the stiffness left his limbs. He screwed his eyes up into a squint and directed his gaze toward the stable yard, but he could see nothing of Evald, so he took himself out to the stable, for further investigation. There was no one there either, so he walked right on through until he came to the cow yard, and there, what did he see but Evald squirting milk into the maw of some creature or another!

"What is this I see?" demanded Ole, coming up behind Evald and taking him by the collar. "I knew it! I knew it!" he screeched. "Any time you become so willing to do what is to be done, there is always something foul in the wind. Where did you get that critter, and what is it, and who told you that you could have it? Hand it here."

Evald trembled and wavered for a second; he was afraid to give the little fellow up, for the old man might wring its head off, even as he did with the stupid cod.

"Give him here!" commanded Ole, and reaching out a long, bony hand, he took the dog by the nape of its neck. "Where did you get him? I said."

In a second, Evald had explained all about finding the dog and was pleading with the Farbro to keep him.

"Keep him?" demanded the Farbro. "Have I not all I can do feeding you, without having a dog to feed, also? If the Laplanders left him out in the woods to starve, he was likely of no account anyway. No!"

"Oh, but Uncle, I will eat less if only I may keep him. I won't eat any breakfast if you will let me have him. He doesn't eat much anyway!"

"No, not *now* he doesn't; but when he grows up he will eat me out of house and home!"

"But when he gets grown up, then I will be older. Then I can hunt and fish and get enough to feed him. Farbro, I will mend the nets, and salt the fish, and dig the peat, or anything else you wish, if only I may keep the dog."

The Farbro considered this bargain for a moment. He knew that it was a good price to pay for such a little, useless-looking creature that likely would die anyway. So he finally conceded that Evald might keep him. "But mind you," said the Farbro, "if he starts eating me out of house and home, out he goes!" With that he glared fiercely at both the dog and his protector, and limped painfully out of the cow yard again.

Evald was so happy to think that at last he had something which was really his own, something which would love him, and something he might love, that he got down on his knees right there in the cow yard and thanked the Lord for letting him keep the little animal, whom he named Lova—meaning "to promise."

That evening when Evald had finished his meal, he took up the bucket of milk he delivered to the old sheep owner down the road. The fisher folk of Arnsdalen called him the old "Land Krabbe," meaning land crab, for of course they could not possibly approve of any one who came into their community and pursued an occupation which did not conform with that of the fisher folk. They had all said he would fail when he took up sheep-raising as an occupation. They sniffed at him and would have nothing to do with him. In spite of this, the old Land Crab could afford to drink cream in his coffee and have fresh milk every day; so, although Ole had sniffed the loudest, he now found it possible, once a week or so, to walk across the heather and say good-day to the old man, and tonight he told Evald that he was going with him.

The Land Crab was at the door to meet them. "Good day, good day," said he. "Come right in."

Then Ole thanked him for the last time they had met. Wiping his feet on the willow door mat he went in, asking how everything was going for the herder.

"Oh," said he, "very poorly. A wolf got into my flock Monday and killed one of the sheep before I could get at it. The lamb she left is a problem, for there is not a sheep that will nurse it. Small wonder, too, when one considers its appetite."

Of course, Ole had known it was going to go thus for the other, but he nevertheless kindly refrained from saying so. "Did you get the wolf?" he asked instead.

"The pelt is hanging on the shed door. For a she-wolf the fur was good too. Might have a look at it," suggested the herder, leading the way to the shed. "Too bad I don't know where her lair is, for she must have a couple of starving cubs. It is bad for anything to starve, even if it is a wolf."

"Ha! That is like you, Jonke," said Ole. "Evald and you should make a pair. He brought a dog home today that the Lapps must have left when they moved. Strangely marked he is, too, for a Lapp dog."

"Well, as long as you are bringing up a dog, you might as well take the lamb home too. If you can bring it up, you may have it," said Jonke to Evald.

Now Ole would have liked to say No to that, but he did not want to have it appear that he was harsh to the boy; neither did he wish to offend the herder, so he said nothing.

Evald was so happy at the remarkable good luck of this day that he was struck dumb. That evening, as he walked across the fields, it seemed that his heart could hold no more joy. When he got home he made a new bed in Bjella's manger, and there the dog and the lamb slept together, side by side. As time passed they shared their meals together, played, slept, and frolicked together, so that for all the world one might have thought they were brothers.

One evening when the boy took his bucket of milk down to the old herder, both dog and the lamb started after him. Evald walked sideways, looking at the two tag-tails he had following him. The dog had now grown so round and fat that he was short of breath, and every time his feet touched the ground he gave a grunt. The lamb had long, ungraceful legs, but they were no longer wobbly. It went hoppety, hoppety through the dust, and Lova had to run as fast as he knew how to keep up. Evald laughed in glee, watching them, and so they came, the three of them, into the yard of the herder.

The sheep commenced to mill about and bleat as Evald came near. They huddled together and cried so fearfully that he opened his mouth in surprise at this unusual conduct.

"Funny faces," he shouted at them, "why make so much fuss just because I have come? Can it be you have forgotten me in the night?"

Jonke knew that bleat. It was a cry of fear. Without waiting to put on his birch-bark slippers he rushed out into the sheepfold.

"What's the trouble?" asked Evald, surprised at the old man's alarm. "What are they afraid of?"

"They have gotten the scent of a wolf," replied the sheep herder, as the animals crowded about him. "You didn't see any wolves on your way up here?"

"Wolves in the daytime?" cried Evald, " 'course not."

It was then that Jonke noticed the lamb and the puppy.

"Evald," cried the old man, pointing at Lova, "where did you get that animal?"

"That is the puppy Farbro Ole was telling you about," answered the boy.

"Puppy?" cried the old man. "That a puppy! It's a wolf cub you have, and no puppy at all!"

"A wolf cub?" cried Evald. "A wolf cub?"

"Yes, that it is. Watch the sheep if you have any doubt," replied the old man, pointing to the agitated beasts that were looking out over one another's shoulders with great, frightened eyes. Their frenzied bleating rent the air, until the boy could scarcely hear the herder's voice.

"Shame on you, long faces," said Evald, "to be afraid of this little one."

"It is the same," said the herder, "whether they are large or small, they still give out the same terrifying wolf scent. Evald, you had better get rid of that cub before he grows up and does damage among the sheep."

They looked down at the cub. He was grinning happily and playing with the lamb. *Baa-ah,* said the lamb, and gave the cub a swat across his nose with a clumsy forefoot. The cub leaped upon him so swiftly the wobbly lamb tumbled over, with Lova on top. There they lay, grinning at each other.

Evald snatched them both up into his arms. "I won't have Lova killed!" he cried fiercely. "I won't have either of them killed. Lova is no wolf. He is a Lapp dog, a reindeer dog, but he is no wolf."

The shepherd was impressed by the antics of the lamb and the cub, and he said, "Well, he is your cub; do as you like with him. As for his being a wolf—there is no doubt about that, for the markings of the wolf cub are always the same. Judging by the locality, he may have been the cub of the wolf I killed, for you found him at about that same time, I recall."

"Don't say that," cried Evald, "for if Farbro Ole learns that he is a wolf, he will kill him! I just can't stand to part with him now!"

The old shepherd looked at him kindly. A dreamy look came into his eyes as he thought of himself as a boy in the wilds of this same Norrland. He recalled how starved his life had been, and how little and ugly the hut he had lived in. He remembered how eagerly he had looked forward to the coming of the lambs in the spring. Then he looked at Evald and realized how very much poorer this boy's life was than even his own had been. He had had a mother, sisters, and brothers; this boy had only a wolf cub and a lamb upon which to center his affections. "Evald," said the old man, "I will not say a word to your Farbro about the cub being a wolf. It may be that since you are bringing him up with a lamb he will change his nature. But keep your eye on him, boy, for blood is stronger than water, nine times out of ten."

Evald seized the old man's hand and shook it to show his thankfulness, then he walked along home, the lamb under one arm, the wolf cub under the other. But that night he did not whistle as he generally did, for he knew that someday there would be a reckoning.

In January Ole left with the fishing fleet for the Lofoten. Evald was overjoyed, for now he need have no fear for at least three months. Still the sheep and the wolf were as good friends as they had been while young. When the nights were especially cold and the logs of the old stable snapped with the chill, often the two of them curled up in a corner together and went to sleep, thus keeping each other warm.

At last the snow disappeared and the earth took on life again. Evald watched fearfully for the Farbro every day. Fearfully, for he felt that when he returned the reckoning would come. The wolf had grown to be immense and bore all the fierce markings of his wild ancestors. Ole knew a wolf when he saw one. There was no mistaking this one. So Evald was fully prepared for the worst.

One spring day Ole returned to the hut unexpectedly. He still had the motion of the sea in his legs, and since he had celebrated a little, too, because of the end of the season, his head was light, and words sat glibly upon his tongue. When he saw the hut, he was seized with a sense of joyfulness, so he broke out into a rollicking fishing song. Evald was busy in the stable, and Lova had been left to watch the hut. He saw the old man coming up the road, but since he was in the middle of it, most of the time, the wolf kept his peace and merely watched him suspiciously, for he knew that any one might walk as they pleased upon the highway. But when the man turned up the path to the house and managed to walk in the flower beds, then Lova would have no more of it. He leaped from the porch and stood before the old man, bristling from nose to tail.

Ole did not recognize Lova. "Herre Gud," cried the old man, "it is a wolf!" With that he whipped out his sheath knife and stood with it gleaming fiercely in the sunlight. But the wolf would not move, and the old man dared neither go forward nor backward.

Bucken, the sheep, heard the angry snarl Lova gave as he leaped off the porch and went to the door to look out. Seeing a stranger there on the walk, he turned to Evald.

"Baa-ah," said the sheep and looked out of the door with his head held high. Evald went over to investigate. When he saw what was up, he cried, "Farbro Ole!"

"Yes! Hurry up, boy, here is a wolf. Get the gun!" cried the old man, shaking with fear. "Get the gun!"

"Lova, come here!" commanded Evald. "Come here!"

The wolf gave the old man a hateful look and circled about him.

"Farbro, that is Lova. You two have forgotten each other," cried Evald, laughing shakily.

"Lova! Lova!" repeated the old man. "He is nothing of the kind. He is a wolf, I tell you, and he almost flew at me! I'll have the dirty, sneaking beast killed! Get the gun for me!"

"It is not here," replied Evald. "Carl Johan borrowed it yesterday and has not returned it yet."

"And hasn't returned it! Drat it! When the gun comes home will be soon enough though. I'll fix him! I'll have his hide for snarling at me. The dirty beast!" He spat to right and left in his fury.

Now it happened that the story of the great wolf had spread over the whole countryside. Everyone wondered at this remarkable beast, which lived and played with a sheep and never forgot to be gentle in his playfulness. The fame of Lova had spread inland to the great Bondegord of Herr Sprisberg. Herr Sprisberg was so rich that when he became sufficiently full of ale he would light his pipe with paper money and shout to the world that there was plenty where that came from. Was it a wonder, then, that he wanted the wolf to help him pass his time away? As soon as he heard of Ole's return, he ordered his fleetest horse and went over to make an offer for the wolf. "I will give you a hundred kronor for the brute," said Sprisberg, "and if that is not enough I will give you more."

"It is not enough, then," said Ole.

"A hundred and ten kronor," offered Sprisberg.

"Maj," said Ole.

"A hundred and twenty-five kronor."

"Not enough yet," said Ole.

"Well then, I will give a hundred and fifty kronor, but not an öre more," said Sprisberg. "Give me the wolf."

"Well, you see," said Ole, "the dog is not mine. It belongs to the boy. I will go and see what bargain I can make with him."

"Evald," said Ole, "where is Lova?"

"I don't know," replied Evald.

"Get him, for Sprisberg wants to buy him and that will save my shooting him." Evald went on with his work and said nothing.

"Get the wolf," said Ole sharply. "Don't you hear me?"

"Farbro Ole," said Evald, "tell Herr Sprisberg that where the wolf goes, there I go too. Unless he will take me too, Lova moves not away from here, for he is mine!"

Ole looked at him appalled, horrified that he should dare to voice his mind in that manner, for the boy never spoke a word against the will of his uncle except where the wolf was concerned.

"Evald!" shouted the old man.

The boy looked him squarely in the eyes, and Ole saw that there was little short of murder the boy would not do for the wolf. He could see that rather than give up Lova, the boy would give up his own home.

"Herr Sprisberg is offering a hundred and fifty kronor for the wolf. You surely are not foolish enough to turn down such an offer!" cried the Farbro.

"I would turn down a hundred times a hundred and fifty kronor!" declared the boy with eyes aflame, and the Farbro thought that he saw something of the wolf in Evald too.

The old man could see that Evald was getting so wrought up there was no use talking to him, so he went out and told Sprisberg to bide his time. Sometime, when the boy was away, he would smuggle the wolf over to him. So with a wink and an oath, the rich Herr Sprisberg took his departure.

But the time never came when Evald went anywhere without Lova; the summer and fall came and went, and once more winter returned to the woods of Norrland, fierce and sullen and cold. The wind churned the ever-falling snow about so wildly that few people ventured outside the door. Rather, they sat about the fire and talked of how it would be when the sea gulls again came shoreward and picked the worms from the fresh furrow, for this was a hardy race which ever looked to the morrow for what the day did not hold.

Christmas came in the midst of the swirling snowfall. To Evald, Christmas meant little else than a spruce tree by the hearth, but since he had never known differently, even that was a great deal.

It was two days before Christmas when Lova and Evald went bounding out across the snow drifts to get a spruce tree. When Evald had cut the tree he wanted, he set out for home. "It is strange that Lova did not wait for me. But then, he must have a little freedom too," Evald assured himself, wiping his nose free of frost. "Uga me! What a night this is going to be," he complained. The snow rose up to his hips. Evald battled to get through it until his breath was almost gone and his legs trembled.

"Hasn't Lova come home yet?" Evald inquired in surprise when he reached home.

Ole raised his spectacles and looked at him sharply. "Hasn't what?"

"Hasn't Lova come home yet?"

"Lova? How should I know where he is? Wasn't he with you?"

"Yes, but he didn't come home with me."

"Well, I guess he can take care of himself!" said Ole, and went back to reading his Bible.

Evald plowed out past the grain house and climbed up on the gatepost down by the stable. There he sat and called and called for Lova—but no Lova came.

"Ja-ha," said Farbro Ole. "The time has come at last. He has responded to the call of the wild in him and gone back to the wolves. I told you so, but you would not listen." Then Ole sighed heavily, thinking again of the hundred and fifty kronor. "It's no use to talk to some people!"

Evald said nothing, merely went from window to window. His eyes searched the smoking snowdunes, but there was nothing there to break the shifting whiteness.

At last he rose and said to the Farbro, "I can't stand it any longer. I am going to take the lantern and go out to look for Lova."

"You are going to do no such thing, by ginginy," said the old man at once, as if he had been expecting Evald to submit that solution before long. "You will do nothing of the kind. Get yourself to bed and forget about that wolf!"

"But Farbro Ole, I can just feel that something has gone wrong with the wolf. I know he needs me."

"Makes no difference what you feel. You are not going out into this storm. So take yourself to bed and stop your whining!"

Evald did. That night a great loneliness filled up the whole soul of the boy. Night seemed to creep along, and morning seemed never to come. He tossed about in his wall bed and moaned sleepily now and again; then he would awaken and sit up in his bed to see if daylight had not come.

As soon as dawn commenced to shorten the shadows, Evald sprang out of bed, lit the fire, and threw upon it a couple of logs. He hung the sooty old kettle upon the fire and filled it three quarters full of water. Silently, then, he slipped into his overcoat and drew the cap down upon his ears. Very quietly he stole out of the door. Fortune was good to him, for the Farbro did not awaken.

He sprang upon his skis, and seizing his ski pole, shot across the heavy crust until it crackled and the snow flew to right and left behind him. When he was far enough from the house so that Farbro Ole could not hear him, he commenced to call, "Lova! Lova!" But there was no answer.

He must have been out a full hour when he heard a faint whimper in the distance. He stopped and listened, then he called again. Once more he heard it. A little clearer it was now, and to the left. As one released from a restraining hand, Evald pushed forward. The twigs slapped at his face as he rushed through the alder groves, but he did not heed. Indeed, he scarcely felt the sting. What was a little thing like that compared with the anxiety he had lived through since the night before!

"Lova!" cried out Evald again. "Lova!"

He heard a feeble bark. It was behind him! He shipped about. Then he saw his wolf! He was caught in a trap!

"Lova, Lova," cried Evald in a sort of frenzy. "Lova, my poor Lova!" He dropped upon his knees and tore at the trap which held the toes of the forepaw in its teeth. But the iron was cold and the spring stiff. It would not give. The wolf opened his mouth and grasped Evald's hand, as if he would help him, but the spring would not give. "The skis," cried Evald, and ran to fetch them. He put one under the trip, the other above. Then he stepped upon the trap with his heavy shoes. Slowly the maw opened, and Lova pulled his mangled paw out. He held it up and whimpered, even as he had whimpered that long-ago summer day when he had struggled out of the brown leaves of the birth grove, half dead with hunger. The blood rushed forth anew over the frozen lump which hung, like a crimson berry, from the tip of his paw. Evald wanted to bind it up, but the wolf would have nothing of it. He licked it, as if that helped to soothe the ache. Then he hopped along on three legs for a distance, until he became so spent that he fell in a heap and panted like a dying thing. But as soon as he regained his breath, he would struggle on again. Evald encouraged him and even tried to carry him, but that he could not, for the wolf had outgrown his arms long before.

When the two of them reached home, Farbro Ole no doubt felt more than a little taken aback for his harshness of the night before. He examined the wolf and did for him all that he knew how to do for frostbitten feet. When he was through he said to Evald, "He will lose two of those toes. I can't save them, but I think I can save the rest of the foot."

Lova lost his two toes, as Ole had said, but his foot was saved and healed rapidly. Soon the wolf was running around on the drifts again, and before long everyone forgot that Lova had had this misfortune—everyone excepting Evald.

That was a hard winter. There seemed nothing for the animals in the wilderness to eat, so they harassed the people who lived in Nordland and carried away every living thing that was not watched.

One day Evald took a run on his skis down to the village to see if there was any mail. No sooner had he left the yard than Ole got out the old horse and hitched him up to the sleigh. Now was his opportunity to sell Lova! When the horse was ready, the old man went to the storehouse and fetched out some frozen fish; then he called to the wolf. He could surely get the scent of that fish, the way it smelled! "Lova!" cried Ole, "Lo-va!" He waited for a while, and listened. Again he called. He stood in the wind, now, so that it would carry the odor of the fish abroad, for it was certain the wolf was about some place, since Evald never allowed him to go to the village with him. Again and again he called, until finally Lova did appear. Ole gave him the fish, slipped the rawhide thong about his neck, and got him into the sleigh. Soon the old horse was taking them over the road, inland. Ole was so engrossed with thoughts of what he was going to buy with the money he would obtain for Lova that he did not notice that the stars were coming out overhead, nor that the winter blue of the sky was deepening and casting lengthy shadows across the narrow, crooked road that wound uncertainly through the birch and alder thickets. Neither did Ole notice as the shadows took form and stealthily approached from every side. He did not, but Lova did.

The wolf sat up in the sleigh and sniffed the air nervously; then the fur on his back stiffened, and he snarled. "Snarling, eh?" demanded the old man. No sooner had he said it than the night air was rent with the blood-curdling howls of wolves. As if the very darkness had bred them, they seemed to appear from all directions at once. Their eyes burned like a thousand fires, flaming and snapping in the savage manner of all wild eyes. "Wolves! Herre Gud! Wolves!" cried Ole, as he scrambled wildly for the fagots [torches] under the seat of the sleigh. He set them in the sockets on the dashboard and fumbled with a trembling hand for the tinder box. It was with difficulty he lighted them, and two more fagots which he waved about over his head frantically, shouting hoarsely at the wolves, who snarled and came nearer.

They had reached a crossroad now. Behind were open fields; before him lay the forest. He must turn back! Ole leaped out into the snow. The horse must be turned about. Already Lova was out, walking before the animal as if to protect him from a front attack. The horse snorted and reared, terrified by the strong scent of wolf in the air. Ole yanked him by the halter to make him move forward, while with the other hand he waved the fagot about. "Lord," he prayed wildly, "save us from the wolves!"

Just then the horse gave another start. Ole slipped and was dashed headlong into a drift. Instantly a wolf was upon him! He shrieked and strove to regain the fagot. The wolf grasped him by the fur collar of his coat and tore frantically until the fur flew. "Lova!" cried the old man. "Lova!" It was not necessary to call, for the wolf had already been upset and Lova was upon him.

Ole, trembling all over, scrambled up. He snatched up the fagot, then he whipped out his sheath knife. He must save Lova! But as if the animals had been one, they whirled about, snarling and tearing at each other. He could not tell them apart. Ole yelled and waved his torch at them, but they only fought on. Now the other wolves were coming nearer, howling hideously! Ole lit another torch and flung it into their midst. They snarled and drew back—all but one, which made a leap at the horse that had backed into a drift. He leaped again. This time Ole's knife caught him. It came out crimson, and the wolf rolled over into the snow, with a smothered snarl. Even as he fell, the pack was upon him. Ole jerked the horse down the road in a wild dash to escape the whirling mass. He sprang back into the sleigh again, and as he did he heard the long-drawn wolf howl of conquest. Could it be that Lova had been killed? That Lova had given his life for him? Not until now did he realize what the wolf had come to mean to him.

He looked about. In the starlit night he saw a beast standing with his nose in the air. The treble of that death cry put despair into his heart—a despair and silent reproach he would ever carry within his breast. What would Evald say when he knew what had happened? How could he tell him that the head of the pack had killed Lova? As he thought this, he heard the cry of the other wolves as they pounced upon the fallen enemy and commenced to tear him asunder, even as he had torn the other. Had it not been for Lova, he, Ole, would now be lying in the place of that wolf. He shuddered, and drawing his cane out he laid it across the horse's back. He must get home before they had finished Lova.

"Where is Lova?" cried Evald, as he tore the traces from the hooks. "He is not gone? He is not killed?" That Ole did not answer, merely hurried the horse along to the stable.

"Farbro Ole," sobbed Evald, as he opened the stable door and latched it, "Farbro Ole, where is Lova?"

The old man could not answer, there was such a lump in his throat!

If the wolf had only done something to warrant this treatment! Why could he not have invaded a sheepfold and slaughtered a couple of sheep as his ancestors had done! Then there would be something as an excuse for his actions.

The Farbro now saw himself as he was. Perhaps he realized how harsh he had been to the boy. What would he not have given to have the wolf back again, and alive!

"Evald, I might as well tell you now as later," he commenced bitterly. "The wolves got him. He died to save me."

For the first time in his life, Ole had nothing further to say. The tears were in his own eyes. He did not dare to trust his voice.

Evald staggered into the manger where the sheep was lying in the dark. He threw his arms about its neck and sobbed as if his heart would burst.

The old Farbro set the lantern upon the floor and sank down on the three-legged milk stool, silently waiting for the tempest of Evald's grief to spend itself. When the boy was sobbed out, the old man took him by the arm and said, far more gently than he had ever spoken to him before, "Evald, my boy, come in now."

Broken with grief, Evald stumbled blindly through the snow back to the hut. Tonight he would have no supper. He would go to bed, where a boy might cry and not have anyone to see him. The wolves had claimed their own, but how they had claimed it!

The boy had scarcely climbed into the bed before a blood-curdling wolf howl of conquest rent the darkness. "It is the one who killed Lova," cried the old man. Again the long, trembling cry pierced the night.

"No," cried Evald. "No! No! No!" Without pausing to dress, he sprang from his bed, unlatched the door, and flung it open so that the firelight fell in a shaft of radiance upon the snow without. A wolf was sitting there, baying to the moon, telling the world about his triumph. "Lova!" cried Evald. "Lova!" And plunging into the snow in his bare feet he threw his arms about the wolf.

The old man stood in the doorway with a new wonder in his eyes. His heart was filled with a deep thanksgiving for from this wolf he had learned to comprehend the unfathomable love and fidelity in the heart of a boy.

* * * * *

"The Boy and the Beast," by Nora Burglon. Published in St. Nicholas, *November 1930. Original text owned by Joe Wheeler. Nora Burglon wrote Scandinavian-based stories for popular magazines during the first half of the twentieth century.*

TOGO, THE SLED DOG
and the Great Serum Run to Nome

Joseph Leininger Wheeler

"The wrong dog got the credit!"
—Leonhard Seppala

* * * * *

This is unquestionably the greatest sled dog story ever told—and it has been told many times, from many different perspectives, but with one constant: the wrong dog gets the credit. And herein lies our story.

PRELUDE

"We are prisoners in a jail of ice and snow. The last boat . . . is gone and this little community is left to its own resources, alone with storms, alone with the darkness and the chill of the North."

—*Nome Chronicle*

Nome is a city that should never have been, for there are few worse places on earth on which to build a town. Even in the 1920s, it was the northwesternmost city in North America. Two degrees above the Arctic Circle on the southern shore of the Seward Peninsula, it is closer to Siberia than to any major town in Alaska. Just a little north, on a clear day, one can look out across the Bering Strait to Russia, only fifty-five miles away. Because the International Date Line is only a few miles from the western-most tip of the peninsula, one could, according to Salisbury, "see tomorrow." In 1925, Seattle was the closest major port, 2,400 miles south.

Summer in Nome was an aberration, as anyone who was asleep at the switch and missed the last ship out soon found out. Of course few did, for if you lacked the necessary funds to get you through seven to eight months of winter, and adequate lodging, the U.S. Army would force you to board the last boat. In winter, dark was a constant (only four hours of subdued light a day). By early November, the Bering Sea would be frozen over till summer. According to Gay and Laney Salisbury, in their riveting best-seller, *The Cruelest Miles,*

> The unrelenting cold would come on suddenly and violently, with bliz-
> zards that lasted for days and brought about an extreme isolation that could
> sap the determination of the hardiest soul. . . . The tundra's rivers and creeks
> would freeze over and the frozen surface would become smooth and trans-
> parent to reflect the night stars like "tips of small torches held up from the
> depths." . . . Out on the Bering Sea, the waves would flatten out as the sea
> turned into thickening sheets of ice. . . . On shore, the floes piled one on top
> of another in towering hummocks. . . . When the blizzards came, one might
> feel "as if an unseen hand were clutching at your throat" (3–8).

So, in such an inhospitable land, how did Nome get here in the first place? The answer takes us back to the Panic of 1893, one of the worst depressions in history, when in the U.S. alone, almost 15,000 companies and 600 banks failed; 20 percent of all Americans lost their jobs. Because the Panic's effects were global and long-lasting, when in 1896, gold was discovered in the Klondike in Canada's Yukon Territory, desperate would-be miners flooded in over the Chilikoot Pass (Alaska) on up to Dawson City. Jack London was one of those gold seekers; he'd find gold, not in the ground but in the pages of his books.

Thus it was that when, two years later, three miners (ever after known simply as the "Three Lucky Swedes") found gold nuggets in the beach sands of Nome, it didn't take but the news of this find to siphon away thousands of miners from Dawson City. Because the only route to get there was via the 2,300 mile-long Yukon River, this emigration of erstwhile Klondike miners was stretched out so far that campfires were rarely extinguished. And because there were precious few human habitations along the way, they had to make their own bread—for which they needed a leaven called sour-dough starter. Because they kept their sourdough starter next to their chests to keep it from freezing, they—and miners everywhere—were soon called "sourdoughs." This first invasion of gold-seekers made the most of Nome's short summer in 1899.

But by the time the ice melted in 1900, more than fifty shiploads of miners and those who knew nothing about mining except what they'd heard (that on the beaches of Nome gold was there just for the picking up) were eager to rush ashore. Most of these were soon dubbed "Cheechakos"—not because they carried yeast but because Alaskans considered them totally ignorant where mining and the polar North was concerned. More than twenty thousand from all over the world (Norwegians, Russians, French, and Americans predominating) now transformed the little hamlet into the Alaska Territory's largest city. Tents stretched along the beach for some thirty miles. There was a veritable babble of languages. Gambling halls and saloons sprang up. Wyatt Earp came—as did Rex Beach, who from the wild times that followed got the idea for the plot of his famous novel *The Spoilers*. Because the sun remained in the sky for twenty hours a day, Nome never slept. Gold dust was exchanged for everything, and player pianos were kept well-oiled. Dance hall girls charged a dollar a twirl, eggs sold for four dollars a dozen, and coal for a hundred dollars a ton. Soon more and more miners were destitute. Crime became rampant: miners armed with knives and guns jumped claims; at night thieves would sneak in, chloroform sleeping miners in their tents, and steal their valuables. Life was cheap.

Fall was already in the air when on September 12, 1900, a terrific storm blew in with seventy-mile-per-hour winds; massive waves wiped out the beach tent-cities, and great waves crashed clear up to Front Street. Many miners were washed out to sea.

As for the aftermath,

> As the waves receded and debris piled up on the shore, thousands of prospectors who had survived months of lawlessness, drunkenness, and poverty, decided they'd had enough. They stood quietly in long lines on the beach and waited for the next ship out. They were called—with reason— "cold feet," and they all had one thing in common: they could no longer bear the thought of another day in Nome.

> By late October, most of the 20,000 men and women who had arrived a few months earlier had shipped out. Someone would later comment that "even God leaves on the last boat out of Nome" (Salisbury, 18, 19).

By all rights, Nome should now have joined the ranks of hundreds of other mining boomtowns that went bust and become desolate ghost towns crumbling back into dust. But when everyone had left but diehards, the diehards kept it alive. Discovery Channel's *Alaska* puts it this way:

> This remote community has long been known as the city that wouldn't die, although it has had more than enough reasons to disappear many times since its founding in 1899. Nome has been burned to the ground [twice], pounded by relentless gales [four times], attacked by flu, diphtheria and countless other maladies; and almost starved out of existence, yet its population has always rebuilt and struggled on (302).

More or less by default, Nome became the commercial hub of the Seward Peninsula and the 10,000 people who lived in the region's scattered villages. But Nome needed something more than that to really flourish again. If only they could figure out a way to capitalize on a home-grown product, such as sled-dog teams.

For a while they thought they'd found the answer, with what they called the "All Alaska Sweepstakes," first run in 1908. It quickly became such a success that Nome became known as the Dog Capital of the World. Once each year's race started, it seemed that all other life in the region went into a holding pattern. At each telegraph station along the way would be someone dubbed the "Information Kid" who would telegraph back to Nome when each team went by, so that spectators and gamblers could keep track of who was leading, and by how much.

Epidemic!

In all that vast peninsula, there was only one doctor, Dr. Curtis Welch. He loved this vast land of Alaska, stretching out across 580,000 square miles (as large as England, Italy, Spain, and France combined); it also has more shoreline than all the rest of the states combined. Dr. Welch even loved it in the winters when so few townspeople remained. But the Native Americans had no place to go, for this was home.

As always, the good doctor had conscientiously and carefully gone through his checklist several times before the last ship, *The Alameda,* left in the fall. For once the ice closed in, there'd be no chance to order medical supplies. He now remembered, this December of 1924, that he'd made sure he had enough of such things: cotton balls, tongue depressors, thermometers, and needed medicines. Most everything he'd ordered had arrived—except one item: his request to the health commissioner in Juneau to send him a fresh batch of diphtheria antitoxin. He had very little of it left, and what he had was already seven years old. Oh well, since in all his eighteen years of practicing medicine in the peninsula, he'd never seen even one confirmed case of that deadly childhood disease, in all likelihood, he wouldn't need it. But still he worried: *How could one know?* (Salisbury, 9).

Even in this remote outpost of civilization, Christmas was Christmas—especially for the town's children. For weeks, shop windows along Front Street had been filled with such things as skates, sleds, dolls, and erector sets.

On Christmas Eve in Eagle Hall, many of the town's two hundred children would be there for the celebration and to see the Christmas tree (stunted though it was), brought in from ninety miles away (the closest available evergreen). The fire in the fireplace would be blazing away, stockings filled with goodies would be hung from the mantel. The choir from the Eskimo church would sing carols in their native tongue, Fire Chief/Santa Claus Conrad Cheney would arrive in a sleigh pulled by two unruly reindeer—oh, it would be wonderful!

But Dr. Welch was puzzled: for some strange reason, ever since *The Alameda* had sailed off, there had been one tonsillitis case after another. And on the morning of December 4, a seven-year-old Eskimo-Norwegian girl, Margaret Solvey Eide, came down with a severe sore throat and fever. But Margaret Eide would miss the festivities this year; each day she grew worse, and on December 28, she died. The case bothered Welch because death from tonsillitis is rare. But the mother refused to permit him to perform an autopsy.

Always in the back of his mind was the terrible Spanish Flu pandemic of seven years before, which had killed more than forty million people worldwide, more than all of World War I. By the time it was over, one out of every two of the Native population of Nome had died. And those who survived now suffered from weakened immune systems.

By January 1925, more disturbing news: two more Native children had died. Welch began to suspect the worst.

Then, on Tuesday afternoon the twentieth, during his hospital rounds, Welch looked in on three-year-old Billy Barnett, checked in two weeks before with a sore throat, swollen glands, fever, and fatigue. Now Billy was worse: thick grayish lesions in his throat and nasal membranes—characteristic of an ancient and dreaded bacterium, a centuries-old killer of young children. For good reason it was often referred to as "the strangler." Its official name: diphtheria. By 4:00 P.M., Welch was certain. All the symptoms of the deadly disease were here: sunken eyes, an expression of unrelenting despair, dark lips the color of wild berries; and each time Billy tried to draw air into his lungs, he coughed up blood. By 6:00 P.M., Billy was turning blue from lack of oxygen. The child's windpipe was so clogged, the doctor could hear a faint high-pitched trill, sounding like someone was slowly letting the air out of a balloon. In only moments, Billy had breathed his last.

Dr. Welch checked his medical journals. Before antitoxin, the death toll from diphtheria was much higher than now (infecting 150,000 in the U.S. annually, killing one out of every ten). Before the antitoxin it had been one of the leading causes of death in the U.S.—especially among young children. It had wiped out entire communities in Europe and the Middle East. In 1735, an outbreak of this "plague in the throat" raged for five years in the American colonies. Some towns lost nearly half of their children.

Next morning, long before dawn, Welch was called to the bedside of another child, seven-year-old Bessie Stanley. When he pried her mouth open, he could smell the stench. The inside of her mouth had become one mass of fetid stinking membrane. By late evening, she, too, would be dead.

Nome was facing a catastrophe of epic proportions. He called the mayor, George Maynard, and asked him to immediately summon the town council into emergency session. There wasn't a moment to lose! (Salisbury, 33–46).

In record time, they'd gathered in his office. There was George Maynard, publisher of the *Nome Nugget* and mayor; Mark Summers, superintendent of the Hammon Consolidated Gold Fields; attorney Hugh O'Neil; and others. Dr. Welch explained the situation in detail to them. They had an epidemic on their hands and only enough serum (most of which was already seven years old) for six patients at the most. To properly fight the epidemic, he needed at least a million units.

Fresh in council members' minds was that terrible flu epidemic of seven years before when over a thousand had died just in Nome. They quickly agreed to lock down the town immediately because diphtheria is extremely contagious. Every school, church, moviehouse, and lodge would be shut down. No child could leave home at all.

Welch then hurried over to the telegraph station and asked the U.S. Signal Corps officer to send out two urgent bulletins: one to be sent all over Alaska, alerting every major town and official, including the territorial governor in Juneau, to Nome's desperate need for serum.

The other would go to Washington, D.C., to Welch's colleagues at the U.S. Public Health Service, which regulated the production of antitoxins and vaccines. This was the telegram:

> An epidemic of diphtheria is almost inevitable here STOP. I am in urgent need of one million units of diphtheria antitoxin STOP. Mail is only form of transportation STOP. I have made application to Commissioner of Health of the Territories for antitoxin already STOP.

In less than a week, Nome's plight would make the front pages of nearly every newspaper in America.

* * * * *

The town was immediately locked down, and any home harboring a diphtheria victim was identified by a big red sign: **QUARANTINE. KEEP OUT.**

The existing serum was used where the need was most urgent. By Saturday, there were at least twenty cases, with at least fifty others still at risk.

The City Council now discussed another major problem: How to *get* the serum once it was found. The Bering Sea was ice-locked. At that time, mail and supplies were transported by ship to the ice-free port of Seward, but that was well over a thousand miles away. But there was rail service to Nenana, 420 miles inland. From there it took about twenty-five days for the mail teams to travel the 674 miles west to Nome.

Mark Summers had a suggestion: the route could be covered by two fast dogsled teams, one starting from the railhead at Nenana heading west, the other from Nome heading east. They'd meet halfway at Nulato. And Summers knew just the man for the western portion of the run: the gold company's main driver; the Norwegian, Leonhard Seppala, had already proved over and over in All Alaska Sweepstakes races to be the fastest musher in Alaska. Seppala's lead dog, Togo, was just as legendary. The council unanimously agreed to proceed accordingly, but the mayor urged them to also explore the possibility of flying the serum in. Maynard immediately telegraphed the one man who had the political clout to make an air rescue possible: Dan Sutherland (Alaska's delegate to the U.S. Congress).

The Race to Nome

Forty-seven-year-old Seppala (known as Sepp to his friends) was considerably larger than life. Also a natural showman, known to flip double-back handsprings and delight children by walking down Front Street on his hands. According to Patricia Chargot, in her book *The Adventures of Balto,* Sepp's early childhood was spent in his native Skjervoy, a Norwegian fishing village 500 miles north of the Arctic Circle. He was only eleven when he was first sent to Alaska to join his father in his fishing enterprise. At Nome he found all the adventure any man could handle, first as a gold prospector, then as a sled dog racer. Sepp and his Siberian huskies had won every big race in Alaska, including the 408-mile All Alaska Sweepstakes three years in a row.

" 'That man is a superhuman,' one competitor said of Seppala. He passed me every day of the race, and I wasn't loafing any. I couldn't see that he drove his dogs. He just clucked [with a sound like *tlk, tlk*] to them every now and then, and they would lay into their collars harder than I've ever seen dogs do before.

"Something came out of him and went into those dogs with that clucking."

According to his wife Constance, the dogs always came first in her husband's life: "Our living room was often a place of utter confusion, littered with mukluks, harnesses, dog sleds, tow lines, ropes, and other equipment being repaired and spliced and generally worked over."

Sepp had raised each of his huskies from pups and knew them as well as he knew his wife and child. The dogs' diet had to contain enough protein and fat to keep them healthy—hence salmon. It would take Sepp all summer to catch the needed five thousand pounds of salmon, cut them up, and hang them up to dry on racks. Besides that, his dogs' health and attitudes had to be monitored daily, for an unchecked virus could easily wipe out the entire kennel.

On the trail, after ten long hours, the dogs had to eat first, taking Sepp two to three hours. Wood chopped and holes hacked through ice for water which was then hauled up to camp, pail by pail, a gallon per dog. Once the feeding was over, Sepp massaged each animal's sore muscles, and spruce boughs were cut for their bedding. The smell and feel of it was a comfort to the tired animals.

This was followed by what mushers call "the thank you howl." One dog would start with a high-pitched dreamlike wail, which would be picked up by one dog at a time, until every dog, nose up, would have joined in. Then, as suddenly as it began, the dogs would turn in ever tightening circles, paw at their bedding, settle down, cover their noses with their tails, and fall asleep.

Only then, did Sepp feel free to address his own needs.

Yet Sepp loved the life—in spite of the tough conditions.

Togo, from the very start, fit no mold. According to Salisbury, he defied the odds at every turn. First, he was one of those rarities: the only pup in the litter. His mother, Dolly, was one of the original fifteen Siberians Jafet Lindeberg purchased from Russia, with the intent of (after they'd been well-trained, of course) gifting them to famed arctic explorer Roald Amundsen, who was planning an expedition to the North Pole. Lindeberg entrusted the training of the Siberians to Seppala, who promptly fell in love with the puppies. A few weeks later, when Amundsen canceled the trip, Lindeberg permanently turned the dogs over to his employee, Seppala. And the rest, as they say, is history, for Seppala's Siberians are considered by Alaskan mushers to be the royal progenitors for the entire breed of huskies. (When speaking of her dogs' lineage, the dog breeder who was our hostess in Juneau [on a recent cruise], lowered her voice reverentially when she solemnly intoned, "They're descended from Seppala Siberians.") Togo's father was Suggen, Seppala's then lead dog. With Suggen, Seppala dominated the All Alaskan Sweepstakes as well as other dog races; and no doubt would have continued to do so had not World War I resulted in the demise of the race.

Seppala initially paid little attention to Togo, for not only was he small for a Siberian, but he also developed an ailment that caused his throat to swell; consequently, Sepp's wife Constance personally ministered to the puppy's needs and continually applied hot compresses in order to soothe the throat-related pain. Despite, or perhaps because of, all this attention, Togo became not only difficult but a real pest: whenever Sepp tried to harness the team, Togo would rush out and nip the ears of the working dogs, resulting in a predictable uproar.

Finally, Sepp had had enough; he gave away the six-month old delinquent. But Togo (named for the famed Japanese admiral, Togo Heihachiro, who won the Russo-Japanese War) had no intentions of settling down as a house dog. Several weeks later, Togo risked serious injury by leaping through a windowpane and returning to his old home. Sepp, feeling that any dog that devoted to his teammates deserved to be accepted back, did so.

The Salisbury cousins (the best source I've found for Togo's story) note that even being accepted back failed to reform the incorrigible pup: he became an escape artist, always managing to get loose and harass Sepp's team on the trail. He'd even attack lead dogs in approaching teams on the trail—or did until a team of veteran malamutes so mauled him that he barely escaped with his life. Togo never made that mistake again.

Togo was about eight months old when he got into trouble again. Sepp had been ordered to Dime Creek, 160 miles away; because it was urgent that he get there quickly, he first made sure Togo would not be able to follow him this time; but that night, Togo not only broke free from his tether, he jumped the seven-foot-high fence, and got one of his hind legs caught in the wire mesh. He squealed like a pig until cut down by a kennel hand; then Togo dropped to the ground, rolled over, and sped off in search of the team.

It took Togo all that night to catch up with Sepp at Solomon. The next morning, there Togo was, harassing the team as usual and leading them away from the trail in order to chase reindeer. Thoroughly exasperated by now, Sepp had no alternative but to slip the harness over Togo's neck and put him in the wheel position at the back of the team so he could keep close tabs on him.

To Sepp's amazement, Togo immediately settled down, focused all his attention on the trail, and kept his tug line taut. *So that's been his problem!* Fascinated by the dog's sudden reformation, as the day wore on, Sepp kept moving Togo up the line.

"By the end of the day, the eight-month-old shared the lead with a veteran named Russky and had traveled seventy-five miles on his first day in harness. It was a feat unheard of for an inexperienced puppy. This was no canine delinquent but an 'infant prodigy,'" Seppala said. "I had found a natural-born leader, something I had tried for years to breed" (Salisbury, 160–162).

According to Robert J. Blake, in his book *Togo,* in 1918, Seppala entered Togo in his first race, the Borden Marathon. The next year they set the record for the fastest time ever in that event. Race after race it was always the same—Togo's team the winners. "Seppala became known as the fastest man in North America. 'It's because of that dog Togo,' everybody said" (Blake, 9).

Most of a dog-lifetime later, Togo was still Sepp's lead dog. According to Salisbury, "The relationship was based on friendship as much as on partnership and mutual need. They were 'inseparably linked,' a friend said. 'One does not speak of one without mention of the other.'" They would often romp together at night, and Seppala's favorite game was to try to grab Togo's feet while the dog danced. If Seppala was tired, he often sat by the fire with the dog next to him.

"Togo simply seemed to know what to do, Seppala once told a reporter. One time, before the start of an eight-mile race, he had hitched the dog up to a sled driven by a young girl who had never ridden before, and he whispered in the dog's ear: 'Go for it. I'll be waiting here for you.'

"Togo sped through the course and headed straight for Seppala, who was kneeling at the finish line. As the two rolled over and wrestled in the snow, a few spectators wiped tears from their eyes.

"Now, as Seppala led the dogs through their drills in the Sawtooth Mountains, he felt lucky to have Togo with him for the round trip to Nulato. Togo had accompanied his master on every important journey, and together they had covered nearly 55,000 miles of trail. They had saved each other's lives many times crossing the frozen Norton Sound, and despite Togo's advanced age, Seppala still felt that wherever they went together, he could travel 'with a sense of security.'

"This time there would be no cash prizes, no records set. They would be saving lives" (Salisbury, 76).

Patricia Chargot, in her *Adventures of Balto,* noted that Alaska's top husky weighed only fifty pounds! But Togo was " 'fifty pounds of muscle and fighting heart,' as Seppala liked to say. He was a natural born leader that, in Sepp's opinion, had the temperament of a genius. . . . Togo had boundless energy and endurance and an unerring sense of the trail, even in the most blinding of blizzards" (Chargot, 13).

* * * * *

Meanwhile, as the entire nation kept tabs with the day-to-day situation in Nome, the wheels were moving: Dr. John Bradley Beeson of Anchorage had come across 300,000 units of antitoxin—and much farther away, the Public Health Services had rounded up 1.1 million units in West Coast states. But Beeson's serum would have a two-week head start.

Back in Juneau, territorial Alaska's governor, Scott C. Bone, was hard at work trying to find the right solution. And the weather wasn't helping. It had turned bitterly cold, bringing territorial travel to a near standstill—in fact, temperatures were at a twenty-year low, and were getting colder yet. Even in Juneau, outside the governor's office were drifts ten feet deep. Terrific blizzards had plated ships with so much ice their captains desperately sought harbors.

As for air travel, with open cockpits, the governor couldn't even imagine a pilot being able to endure temperatures of minus 50 degrees. After all, in a recent test, with temperatures of minus 10 degrees, the pilot had to put on so much winter clothing, the plane had been virtually unflyable. As for the water-cooled engines, they'd never even been tested in such bitterly cold temperatures; and anti-freeze hadn't even been invented yet. And there were no recognizable landmarks or radio systems to guide the pilot to the destination; there was no weather forecasting to warn him of storms; there were no airports; and most crucial of all: there was only four hours of semi-light to see by in polar night.

Yet, offsetting all this was the desire of many Alaskans to use this opportunity to boost Alaskan air travel while all the world was watching.

By late January 26, Governor Bone arrived at a decision: the serum had to be taken to Nome by dogsled. But instead of sending one team to meet Seppala midway on the trail as originally planned, he'd set up a relay of the best and fastest drivers to be found. The teams would travel night and day until they met up with Seppala at the halfway mark.

In 1925, the airplane had not been built that could match the endurance, speed, and reliability of men and dogs.

* * * * *

Now Governor Bone ordered Dr. Beeson to hand-deliver the precious serum to the train officials. Beeson used cork or rubber stoppers so the serum could safely expand without breaking the vials. He wrapped a heavy quilt around the cylindrical serum container, then covered the wooden crate with a thick brown cloth. Afterward, he warned the train-master to pass the word along that once the serum reached the traildrivers, they were to warm up the serum at every stop to keep it from freezing. Then it was on its way.

At Nenana, there would still be 674 miles to go.

The 1925 Serum Run participants

The following is the generally accepted order of the mushers in the first serum run, as well as the mileage they covered.

MUSHER	RELAY	LEG	DISTANCE
Jan. 27, 28	"Wild Bill" Shannon	Nenana to Tolovana	52 miles
Jan. 28	Edgar Kalland	Tolovana to Manley Hot Springs	31 miles
Jan. 28	Dan Green	Manley Hot Springs to Fish Lake	28 miles
Jan. 28	Johnny Folger	Fish Lake to Tanana	26 miles
Jan. 29	Sam Joseph	Tanana to Kallands	34 miles
Jan. 29	Titus Nikolai	Kallands to Nine Mile Cabin	24 miles
Jan. 29	Dave Corning	Nine Mile Cabin to Kokrines	30 miles
Jan. 29	Harry Pitka	Kokrines to Ruby	30 miles
Jan. 29	Bill McCarty	Ruby to Whiskey Creek	28 miles
Jan. 29	Edgar Nollner	Whiskey Creek to Galena	24 miles
Jan. 30	George Nollner	Galena to Bishop Mountain	18 miles
Jan. 30	Charlie Evans	Bishop Mountain to Nulato	30 miles
Jan. 30	Tommy Patsy	Nulato to Kaltag	36 miles
Jan. 30	Jackscrew	Kaltag to Old Woman Shelter	40 miles
Jan. 30, 31	Victor Anagick	Old Woman Shelter to Unalakleet	34 miles
Jan. 31	Myles Gonangnan	Unalakleet to Shaktoolik	40 miles
Jan. 31	Henry Ivanoff	Shaktoolik to Seppala handoff just outside Shaktoolik	
Jan. 31	Leonhard Seppala*	Shaktoolik to Golovin	91 miles
Feb. 1	Charlie Olsen	Golovin to Bluff	25 miles
Feb. 1	Gunnar Kaasen	Bluff to Nome	53 miles
Total Miles: 674			
Total Time: 127 hours 30 minutes (5 ½ days)			

*Leonhard Seppala drove 170 miles to Shaktoolik to meet the serum team, plus the 91 miles to Golovin, for a total of 261 miles (over five times that of any other driver!) On one day alone, Togo led his team across 84 miles.

Nor did Alaska railroad men have it easy in those days. According to the January 31, 1925, Anchorage *Daily Alaskan,* "Blizzards often blocked the tracks, and the cold temperatures created frost heaves and an icy coat over the equipment. The old locomotives, built in 1906, were originally intended for Panama, so the engine car where coal was shoveled into the firebox was open and unprotected from the elements. 'These storms are of such severity that they have often blown the windows out of the engine cabs and sent our men to hospitals for months with pneumonia,' a railroader told reporters in January 1925. Many times engine men have been lifted bodily from their open cabs, being so overcome with cold as to be incapable of moving."

So just imagine what it must have been like to the engine crew in the minus 50 degree below zero weather they braved in order to get the serum through to the drop-off point.

The Great Serum Run

Waiting for the train at Nenana was "Wild Bill" Shannon. He'd been picked to anchor the first (and one of the longer legs) of the serum run for good reasons: he was a mail driver, miner, trapper, and fearless dog driver, and known to have the fastest dogs in that area. Though known to be a daredevil, he could be deadly serious about weather conditions he might face. And he was mighty serious now. For the temperature was dropping well below the minus 30 to 40 degrees below zero that was typical for the time of year. When it got this cold, your breath formed into ice crystals and the air pinched your nostrils as you drew it in. It was like the sting of a bee, and the pain cut short every deep breath.

If he ventured out onto the trail, he'd be violating one of the most sacred laws of the North: never go out and risk your life and that of your dogs in abnormally cold or hot weather—it was called the "rule of the 40s." At 40 degrees and over, a husky risks overheating and dehydration because of its thick double coat of fur; at minus 40 degrees, 2 degrees below the point where mercury freezes, there is little room for error. Tonight it was minus 50 below zero and still falling.

Salisbury notes that "in any weather condition, mushing was a dangerous profession: a sweeper (low-hanging branch) might knock out an unsuspecting driver, moose were known to attack and kill dog trains and their drivers without any provocation; a driver might be stranded without food or supplies. He might get wet, soak his matches, and be unable to build a fire—death awaited him at every turn of the trail, but at minus 40 to 50 degrees, his odds grew prohibitive." At minus 50, a lost glove meant a lost hand. Within minutes any exposed flesh would freeze and turn into the texture of wood. And Shannon knew that only a couple of years earlier, on this same trail, a trapper named Meyers, at minus 50 degrees, had fallen through ice. Shivering uncontrollably, he was unable to light a match; within seconds his face began to freeze. Somehow he blindly stumbled the mile and a half to a telegraph office; when he got inside, his falling to the floor sounded like lumber—he ended up losing both legs.

Shannon's lead dog was Blackie, a five-year-old husky with a white cross on his chest, but his other dogs happened to be relatively inexperienced—and it was a run that normally took two days, with a stop in the middle (Salisbury, 139–141).

Suddenly, the distant chugging of a locomotive could be heard. It arrived, and even before it had stopped, conductor Frank Knight jumped onto the platform and handed the precious cargo to Shannon, who tied it securely to his sled, mounted his runners, and bolted down the trail.

The trail was in atrocious shape, due to deep holes made by a recent horse team dragging heavy freight over it. Finally, Shannon, realizing that he risked incapacitating his dogs on such a trail, ordered Blackie to veer left, out on the frozen Tanana River, which would be even colder than the trail—but he had no choice. And traveling on frozen rivers was more than a little dangerous.

Suddenly Blackie swerved, causing Shannon to momentarily lose his balance—Blackie had just saved them from falling into a black hole big enough to have swallowed the entire team. Shannon's legs started to freeze and his face was growing numb. So he stopped the team, raced to the front, just ahead of Blackie, and began to jog, in order to restore his circulation—which did, for a while. But each time he repeated the process he was proportionally weaker; he knew he was now in danger of hypothermia, for a human can shiver for only so long; soon he'd lose muscle control, sleep would overcome him, and he'd die. Which he knew would happen if he didn't get to Campbell's roadhouse in Minto soon, where he could warm up.

At around 3:00 A.M., Johnny Campbell heard him stumble into his cabin, took one look at him, and was appalled: parts of Shannon's face had turned black from frostbite, and blood stained the mouths of Bear, Cub, Jack, and Jet. The thermometer read minus 62 degrees!

It took four hours of hot coffee before Shannon could regain his equilibrium. Meanwhile he warmed up the precious serum. When he was finally able to check on the condition of his dogs, it was clear that several were suffering from a condition mushers called "lung scorching" (pulmonary hemorrhaging). The lungs fill up with blood. If he continued to Tolovana, in spite of his own condition, it would be without the help of those suffering dogs. But he'd given his word. He left three of them behind and hoped Bear would make it. He was now down to six dogs.

Somehow Shannon made it, but it would be weeks before he could touch his face with a razor. By the time he got back home, three of his dogs would be dead, with Bear dying as well.

Edgar Kalland had been waiting; at 11:00 A.M.—it was still minus 56 degrees, when he set out on the next leg of the journey.

* * * * *

Meanwhile, more than 700 miles north, Leonhard Seppala had left his cabin in Little Creek near Nome with twenty of his dogs. His would be by far the longest leg to travel, and he left under the assumption that he'd have to travel 315 miles to Nulato and 315 miles back—but, unbeknownst to him, orders changed after he was on the trail (there were no telegraph stations on that route, so he wasn't informed). A crowd was out to watch Togo as he led the long team, running at top speed, through the streets of Nome. Sepp had only one major worry—what would he do when they reached treacherous Norton Sound three to four days from then?

* * * * *

Because, with twenty different sled teams participating in this race to Nome, the overall epic is way too long for a short account like this, we are forced to leave out most of the mushers who heroically risked their lives to get the serum through.

* * * * *

Norton Sound. Unquestionably the most dangerous—by far!—part of the serum run. Salisbury captures the drama of this moment better than anyone else:

> Early Saturday morning on January 31, the fourth day of the relay, two
> men—Myles Gonangnan, a full-blooded Eskimo, and the Norwegian Leon-
> hard Seppala—stood on opposite sides of Norton Sound, unaware of each
> other's location, and studied the ice and the wind. They each had a decision
> to make. They could take an over-water route, thereby cutting off a great deal
> of time, or they could follow an onshore trail that skirted the sound. In either
> direction, the trail route was safer, and Seppala had already been warned not
> to attempt an ice crossing. For neither man would the decision be based on
> courage or even stamina—but solely on which way the wind blew.

Over the past few days, the wind had been blowing onshore, pushing water in from the Bering Sea and raising the level of the sound, which had weakened the ice. But as long as the wind continued to blow from that quarter, there would be little cause for alarm. The ice would continue to break up, as it always does, but it would merely drift toward shore. But sometime during the night, the wind's direction had shifted. It was now blowing offshore, from the northeast, and getting stronger.

A little before five o'clock that morning, Gonangnan had received the serum at Unalakleet from his fellow Eskimo and townsman, Victor Anagick, who had traveled down from the Old Woman shelter cabin on the portage. Leaving it inside Traeger's store to warm near the heat of his iron stove, Gonangnan set out to examine conditions on Norton Sound. A few minutes beyond Unalakleet, he would have to decide whether to take the trail route northeast into the foothills or the shortcut route over the ice. The ice route ran several miles out from shore and under the shadow of Besboro Island, an enormous, uninhabited crag that had long ago broken off from the mainland bluffs.

The shortest route of all would have been to cut straight across the sound, which meant heading northwest in a direct line to Nome. But in the middle of the sound was a large body of open water called a polynya, which was kept free of ice most of the season by a constant eddying. As ice formed in the area of the polynya, wind and current pushed it toward the edge, where it compacted and was then driven into the southerly moving ice pack of the Bering Sea. It made a terrifying grinding noise, like that of giant bulldozers dragging their metal buckets against concrete.

Gonangnan studied the giant field of ice as it creaked and sighed, and by the light of the moon he could see the whole body slightly rise and fall. The sea was rolling in from beneath. Somewhere out in the distance there was open water, spray exploding off whitecaps and floes rumbling and fragmenting. In the cavernous sky above, the stars twinkled with unusual clarity. Behind him, the wind was growing stronger, the gusts more frequent. The signs were clear: a storm was brewing and could well land full force on the coast within twenty-four to forty-eight hours. The question was no longer whether the sea would break up but when. He would not risk taking the shortcut.

Gonangnan returned to the store, picked up the serum, and tied the package down in his sled. It was about five-thirty in the morning when he took off for the foothills behind Unalakleet. A few hours later, across the sound, Leonhard Seppala, unaware that the relay had changed, made his decision (Salisbury, 199–201).

* * * * *

Three days after leaving Nome, Sepp neared the dreaded Norton Sound, 150 miles long and 125 miles wide—known to Alaskans as the "ice factory." From a distance, it appeared to be an endless expanse of solid ice; only as you got close would you realize the ice was in a constant state of change and re-creation. Huge swaths would suddenly break free and drift out to sea or a long narrow lead of water would open up and widen. Depending on the temperature, wind, and currents, the ice could assume various configurations—five-foot-high ice hummocks, a stretch of glare ice, a continuous line of pressure ridges, which look like a chain of mountains across the sound. Not surprisingly, Norton Sound was considered the most perilous kind of terrain to cross.

Then there was the wind, a horrendous force that could beat you back instead of permitting forward progress, blowing at speeds of over 70 miles per hour. It could flip sleds, hurl a driver off the runners, and drag the wind chill down to minus 100 degrees. Even more terrifying, when the east winds blew, the ice growing out from the shore often broke free and was sent out to sea in large floes.

Nevertheless, because of the urgency of the need, Sepp and Togo made that perilous crossing. Once on land again, Togo stepped up the pace. Sepp had covered nearly 170 miles in the past three days and so far had been lucky. According to his calculations, he still had over 100 miles to go before he reached the serum, so he was traveling rapidly on. Suddenly, there was a commotion up ahead—another sled-dog team! And the driver was flailing his arms. But Sepp, not expecting to meet any serum run team this soon, urged his team on: "Hup! Hup! Faster! Faster!" Then "*Ssk! Ssk!* Run through!" (Blake, n.p.). Then, at the last minute, Sepp heard the shouted words: *The serum! The serum! I have it here!* It was Ivanoff. At first Sepp could not believe his ears, for he had not known that the epidemic had been growing so rapidly since he'd left Nome that more drivers had been added to the relay in order to speed it up. Sepp had already taken a huge risk and crossed Norton Sound on ice, thus shortening the distance to Nome by a day. Now, he learned he was supposed to carry the serum back across Norton Sound and then on to Golovin, where Charlie Olsen was waiting for the handout.

Alarmed, Seppala lashed the serum to his sled and headed north. Alarmed because Norton Sound had become much more dangerous since his morning crossing. And the wind was steadily increasing. But what option did he have? With things getting worse by the minute in Nome, he made the decision to risk crossing the sound again in order to get the serum to Nome sooner—*if* he made it across, that is. It was now completely dark, the temperature was minus 30 degrees, but with gale-force windchill, it was a brutal minus 85 degrees!

Once before, Sepp had been out on this sound with Togo in a gale like this. A few miles offshore, he'd heard an ominous crack; he ordered Togo to change course, but Togo had already done so and was racing back to shore. Suddenly, Togo inexplicably reared up and somersaulted back onto his teammates. Sepp was angry at Togo's "antics" until he realized the water gap was widening. *They were on an ice floe heading out to sea!* There was nothing he could do but curl up with his dogs, conserve his strength and warmth, and hope a shift in the wind would bring him back to shore.

As hours passed, Sepp's anguish grew. Then Togo gave a short yelp—he'd sensed a shift in the wind. Nine hours later, the shoreline appeared only a few hundred yards ahead. As they neared an ice floe still attached to land, Sepp realized the space between was too wide to jump, but if he could get Togo across, the dog could pull the two floes together. So he tied a long towline to Togo's harness, picked him up, and hurled him across the open channel. Once on the other side, Togo dug his nails into the floe and lurched toward shore—*then the line snapped!* Togo spun around and looked back across the chasm at Sepp. The severed line slipped into the sea. Sepp was speechless. *He had just been given a death sentence.*

Then, unbelievably, Togo sized up the situation: he leaped off the floe, snapped up the line with his mouth, and struggled back onto the icefloe. Holding the line tightly in his jaws, Togo rolled over the line until it was twice looped around his shoulders—then began to pull. The distance narrowed until it was close enough for Sepp and the team to jump safely across! (Salisbury, 209, 210).

Enough of the remembering: the die was cast—if he floated out to sea, it had just been a risk he felt compelled to take. Once more, in the face of gale-force wind and minus 85 degree wind chill—and total darkness—Togo represented the difference between life or death, both for him and the town of Nome. Sepp instinctively knew it would be the last time he and Togo would make this perilous crossing together, for Togo's twelve years made him old in dog years. But in an emergency like this one, Togo was the one dog he was willing to trust his life to. And well Sepp knew that not many mushers would be foolhardy enough to attempt the crossing on a tempestuous night like this.

It was late afternoon, Saturday, January 31, when Sepp stepped onto Norton

Sound. He'd never forget the hours that followed. He could only hold on, unable to see a thing, deafened by the screaming wind, and listening for the sound of cracking ice. But through it all, Togo appeared unfazed, covering mile after mile with head held low, every canine sense straining to fever-pitch. Despite hummocks and slippery patches of ice, he steered as straight a path across the sound as though he and the team had been on rails.

According to Blake, once Seppala noticed the team was slowing down, he ordered a halt, felt his way up the line, discovering that stomachs were beginning to freeze where fur was thinnest. So he worked his way up the entire line, massaging each dog's stomach with his bare hands.

Inch by inch the team worked its way across the bay. Suddenly the wind kicked the sled on its side. The big dog Jens went down, a line twisted around his neck. Dogs scrambled in all directions, pulling the line taut. Seppala made a grab for the line and a dog made a lunge for his arm. Togo barked. The dogs backed off. Seppala loosened Jens and untangled the lines. Then they were off again. . . . Later, Jens collapsed again and was dragged a quarter mile. . . . The eyes of the dog called Johnson froze shut. Seppala cleared them using his own breath (Blake, n.p.).

Suddenly, Sepp realized they'd reached land again. They were on the other side of the sound. The dogs had traveled an incredible eighty-four miles that day, half of it meeting the terrible wind head-on, yet Togo and the team had averaged eight miles an hour.

At 2:00 A.M., Sunday, February 1, Nichuk, the owner of the Isaac's Point roadhouse shook Sepp awake. The storm they knew was coming was already there, so he had no time to lose. Much of the trail between Isaac's Point and Golovin was a few miles offshore; Sepp decided to instead remain within a few hundred feet of land. It was minus 40 degrees, plus windchill as he stepped down the bank. The ice he'd crossed the day before had already broken up, and ominous cracks appeared everywhere. Water spurted up between cracks and the ice heaved. Togo alternated between zigzagging around weak spots and racing toward the safety of the shore. At times blizzard conditions kept Sepp from seeing anything—only Togo knew where they were going.

Finally, they reached shore again—*only a few hours later, the entire section of ice over which they had come broke up into chunks and blew out to sea!*

Once firmly on shore, Sepp stopped the team, rubbed each dog down, brushed off the layer of ice and snow that had formed over their faces, dried off their paws and tended to cuts on their feet. Then he stood up; the most physically challenging part of the fifty-mile segment was still ahead.

According to Salisbury, "Many mushers consider that climb over a series of ridges to the 1200-foot summit of Little McKinley to be the toughest part of the trail to Nome. The exposed ridges stretch out over eight miles. The down grades are steep and the dogs and drivers have little time to recover from one ridge before they have to breathe in deep and charge up the next. By the time the summit of Little McKinley is reached, the team will have climbed about 5,000 feet! Seppala's dogs were being asked to make the climb with less than five hours rest, and after they had traveled for four and a half days and covered 260 miles of trail. With few reserves to call on, the team began to stumble from exhaustion. But they did not stop" (Salisbury, 214).

Now they arrived at their destination in Golovin and passed the serum to Charlie Olsen. Since Sepp had picked up the serum from Ivanoff on the shore ice of Norton Sound, he and his dogs had traveled 91 miles, besides the initial 170 miles. And this was done at top speed, in blizzard conditions, over heaving ice.

* * * * *

Meanwhile, 58 miles from Nome, at Bluff, Gunnar Kaasen waited for the serum to arrive. He'd arrived here sixteen hours earlier so his team was well rested. His team consisted of thirteen dogs; because he didn't own a team himself, he'd borrowed these from his friend Seppala—including the dog Kaasen chose to lead his team—Balto. Even though Sepp considered Balto to be too slow to make his string—he'd had him neutered, in fact—Kaasen liked him anyway.

Olsen finally arrived. It had taken him four and a half hours to travel the 25 miles from Golovin to Bluff. With the wind chill well below minus 70 degrees, putting on the dog blankets had nearly cost him his fingers. The wind had repeatedly blown his team off the trail. Once a hurricane gust of wind had picked up Olsen and his team and hurled them into a nearby drift—it took him some time to extricate himself and the buried dogs.

Ignoring suggestions to wait until the wind died down a bit, Kaasen headed out to face the 70-mile-per-hour wind head on. Once Balto ran right into a towering snowdrift. Kaasen had to extricate the team and return the way they'd come, hoping that since a dog's sense of smell is at least 600 to 700 times greater than a man's, Balto would be able to smell the trail a foot deep in the snow. Balto *was* able to find it.

Several times, the dogs and sled were hurled off the trail. Once, when Kaasen found himself in a snowdrift, he almost panicked—*the serum was gone*! Finally, he found it buried in the snow. But had it been buried farther away, he most likely would never have found it.

At Port Safety, Kaasen had been instructed to turn the serum over to Ed Rohn, who would, in turn, take the serum the last 20 miles to Nome. And it is at this juncture that the most controversial and far-reaching decision of the entire serum race took place. Once it was made, it could not be undone.

According to Kaasen's story, when he arrived at Port Safety at 3:00 A.M., it was dark (Ed Rohn had mistakenly assumed that Kaasen would be waiting at Solomon for the storm to subside before moving on). Then Kaasen just decided to ignore orders and keep going. He arrived in Nome at 5:30 A.M., two and a half hours later. It was Monday, February 2.

Witnesses to the drama of his arrival said they saw Kaasen stagger off the sled and stumble up to Balto, where he collapsed, muttering, "Damn fine dog" (Salisbury, 217–225).

How it all played out

Forever after, many if not most Alaskans (including Seppala) felt Kaasen's ignoring orders was a deliberate effort on his part to steal all the glory from Seppala and the others. Certainly, he deprived Ed Rohn from being a part of one of the greatest sagas in the history of the West. For Dr. Welch and his team thawed out the serum—the vials were still intact, and the serum helped to halt the progress of the epidemic.

Later that day, Kaasen's entry into Nome was reenacted for the press—and that was it: for all across the nation flashed the news and photos of Kaasen and Balto. Both became instant celebrities. Balto would be taken to Hollywood, where Sol Lesser made him into a movie star. Kaasen would embark with Balto on a triumphal tour across the nation. Balto would have his statue put up in New York's Central Park, where it draws crowds to this day. *And there Balto wears Togo's hard-earned racing awards!* Awards Balto never earned. Later on, Kaasen would abandon Balto and other serum-run dogs while on tour; almost they died in a hellish ten cent freak show in California before a kind-hearted Cleveland businessman rescued them and took them to Cleveland, where they lived out their last days.

According to Seppala, *they chose the wrong dog.* For starters, he didn't believe Kaasen's story about not wanting to wake Ed Rohn. He suspected that Kaasen, knowing that news of Nome's plight had captured the world's attention, had simply seen an opportunity and taken it. Why not let Rohn sleep and victoriously deliver the serum himself? There was no glory in being the second-from-the-last man to carry the serum.

"To make matters worse, reporters had credited Balto with Togo's achievements.

Now Balto was glorified as the super Siberian—the veteran racer, skilled navigator, loyal leader that never stopped pulling (all qualities Togo had richly earned—and Balto had not).

"But that wasn't what upset Sepp the most. Togo had run himself to exhaustion on the relay and had badly injured a leg. He would never be able to race again or be able to go on a long run. He would have to retire as Sepp's best leader ever. The sad realization hit Sepp like an icy snowball to the heart" (Chargot, 16).

But time has a way of sorting things out. Though Balto continues to be immortalized by many of the uninformed, where it matters most—in the great state of Alaska—Seppala and Togo gain in stature with every year that passes. Indeed, they are approaching mythical greatness.

On December 5, 1929, at sixteen years of age, Togo's eyes closed for the last time. In a *New York Times Magazine* was this eulogy:

> Every once in a while a dog breaks through the daily routine of feeding and barking and tugging at the leash, and for some deed of super-canine heroism wins the adoring regard of every one who hears of him. His was the kind of life that catches men by the throat and sets them to hero worshiping.

According to Salisbury, as long as he lived, Seppala kept Togo's spirit alive. One reporter put it this way: "In the depths of his [Seppala's] keen gray eyes—lives a dog who will never leave." Writing in his journal at eighty-one, were these words, "And when I come to the end of my trail, I feel that along with my many friends, Togo will be waiting" (Salisbury, 252, 253).

"Togo was the best dog that ever traveled the Alaska trail."
—Leonhard Seppala

* * * * *

And every year, the route of the Great Serum Run to Nome is re-enacted in the greatest race on earth—the Iditarod.

* * * * *

"Togo, the Sled Dog and the Great Serum Run to Nome," by Joseph Leininger Wheeler. Copyright © 2010. Printed by permission of the author.

Sources used:

Anchorage *Daily Alaskan* (Jan. 31, 1925).

Blake, Robert S., *Togo* (New York: Philomel/Penguin Putnam, 2002).

Brown, Tricia, ed., *Iditarod Fact Book* (Kenmore, Wash.: Epicenter Press, 2006).

Chargot, Patricia, *The Adventures of Balto* (Anchorage, Alaska: Publication Consultants, 2006).

Alaska Insight Guide (Melksham, UK: APA Publications, 2009).

Freedman, Lew, *Father of the Iditarod: the Joe Redington Story* (Kenmore, Wash.: Epicenter Press, 1999).

Kimmel, Elizabeth Cody, *Balto and the Great Race* (New York: Random House, 1999).

"1925 Serum Run to Nome," *Wikipedia, The Free Encyclopedia.*

"Nome, Alaska," *Wikipedia, The Free Encyclopedia.*

Rozell, Ned, "Sled Dogs Were Lifesavers in the Serum Run," Geophysical Institute, University of Alaska Fairbanks.

Salisbury, Gay, and Laney Salisbury, *The Cruelest Miles* (New York: W. W. Norton & Company, 2003).

Schultz, Jeff, *Dogs of the Iditarod* (Seattle: Sasquatch Books, 2003).

Standiford, Natalie, *The Bravest Dog Ever: The True Story of Balto* (New York: Random House, 1989).